CARNALLY ROCKS

CARNALLY ROCKS

Peter Murphy

Book Guild Publishing
Sussex, England

First published in Great Britain in 2011 by
The Book Guild Ltd
Pavilion View
19 New Road
Brighton, BN1 1UF

Typesetting in Garamond by
Keyboard Services, Luton, Bedfordshire

Printed in Great Britain by
CPI Group (UK) Ltd, Croydon, CR0 4YY

A catalogue record for this book is available from
The British Library

ISBN 978 1 84624 659 3

Preface

This book started out as a handwritten manuscript. That was back in the 1930s – the best part of 80 years ago. In due course the author, Father, transformed it into hard copy in the late 40s/early 50s using a portable typewriter. Its whereabouts, or indeed its very existence, was not known until it came to light just recently.

It is in fact Father's life story; a veritable human triptych, and read back in the 40s/50s it would have been interesting enough. With the further passage of time and the ever-increasing pace of change, it might now be regarded as a historical document, or in current parlance, social history.

His personal goal was to be an author. In this he really was not successful although he did have articles published occasionally. (See page 201 in the Appendix.) He wrote poems about his beloved 'Carnally Rocks' and amongst his bundle of papers is a play 'From a School Corner' (a clue to his ultimate occupation). He kept a spasmodic diary for most of his life on which no doubt much of this book is based.

It is very much the story of *his* life, not of his family but those with whom he became involved outside his family. In 1920 he met Ethel at the Pink & Lily, a pub near Princes Risborough, where he was endeavouring to become an author. They married and had three children: Sheila Rosaleen, Peter Brendan and James Ciaran.

As to the title, it seems he had two in mind initially: *Carnally Rocks* and *Fools Faring*. Carnally, in South Armagh, the area much in the headlines for some 30 years from 1970 to 2000 as a result of intense IRA activity, was widely known as 'Bandit Country'.

His manuscript has surfaced after all these years. It is perhaps somewhat delayed but we feel duty bound to have it published so that at last he is an author.

Peter Brendan Murphy

1

As I begin this retrospect of my life, I see a thatched cabin under one of those many hills that are an outcrop of the Southern or Carlingford range of the Mountains of Mourne. I see myself climbing that hill to the little plateau on its summit, 'The Green Rock', and from it I gaze wonderingly at the sea to which these mountains roll down. Massively stands out Slieve Gullion, sloping its giant shoulder into the lesser outlines of the mountains of County Louth, from whose feet wind silver-like threads of rivers to be lost in the glistening expanse of water that is Dundalk Bay. Stretched out before me is the scene of the great Irish legends: the mountain slopes on which hunted Finn and the other heroes of the Red Branch Knights; the shore from which Ossian made his great adventure into the Land of Youth; the great plain over which Cuchulain stormed in defence of Ulster.

Beneath the hill was our home, a poor one, a 'room' and a kitchen surrounded by some tumble-down outhouses. The kitchen was the nobler of the two by far. Indeed, as the memory of it flashes back to me after more than sixty years, I realise there was something splendid about it. The wind howls and the rain beats on a winter's night. The hearth is heaped with turf aglow: the bog-oak rafters, glistening with the smoke and soot of over a hundred years, are dancing jade; bath-bricked tin and well-rubbed delft are pools of light. Perhaps a neighbour is in on his ceilidh: jest and story flicker through the shadows. Perhaps my father, in one of his more amiable moods, has me on his knee and is telling me the bardic tales and legends of Ireland. He was the last great repository of Gaelic culture in our district, speaking both Gaelic and English with equal fluency so that he was called 'The Speaker'. And how he could tell those tales! The grave and the gay among them, he had word perfect, handed down to him through centuries of so-called illiteracy.

On the fire bubbled the supper pot, oatmeal porridge taken with buttermilk, or potatoes eaten with buttermilk and, sometimes, as a great treat, a piece of Spanish onion.

The pot would hang on a soot-encrusted crook, which was as crooks go, rather unsatisfactory, refusing to swing as a good crook should, often breaking. My grandfather would then look solemnly at it and curse it as 'Lord Clatterbag's crook'.

'Clatterbag' was long a mysterious term to me. Its English equivalent is 'Gasbag'. Years later when my mother was bewailing me as the plaything of demons she explained to me what was the allusion in the word 'Clatterbag'.

Clatterbag had indeed been a Lord. At the end of the eighteenth century my great-grandfather had been one of the lord's servants. Comely and manly of form had been the servant, and the lord's daughter had signified to him that she would like him to be hers. He made her his honestly enough, but they had to fly far from her father's wrath. I do not know whether they pinched the crook at their elopement or whether it had been donated to them by the lord as his estimate of the son-in-law thus thrust upon him. He was a man who had made a name for himself in Irish politics, but on the wrong side at a time when Ireland had Grattan and Flood as its chief experts in the slinging of words. 'Clatterbag' was the grandson's estimate of his grandfather.

Round about these buildings stretched eight acres of alleged farmland. Furze-covered rocks would account for half of the eight. Perhaps there were two acres of them from which an English farmer would attempt to wrest a crop. Much of what passed for arable land had to be ploughed uphill so that the soil might be kept on the steeply shelving surface. Said one of our local rhymesters, for the tradition or verse, if not of poetry, survived the substitution of Gaelic by English:

On the gorse-clad hills around me the waning sunshine
    floats
Nature meant such land for foxes, for the rabbits and the
    goats:
Surely God, provoked by Adam, never meant that man
    should strive
On such barren soil as this is to keep himself alive.

I have seen my mother carry up soil from the hollows and
spread it over the denuded rocks. In the little spaces so covered
might be grown a few sheaves of oats or a few stalks of potatoes,
and these might stop the hunger wails of her children. My eyes
grew misty as, watching 'Man of Aran', I saw the islanders struggle
with their rocks. Their struggle was the struggle of my people in
a slightly different way.

My father had a further six acres, but they were five miles
distant from our home, and all of them that were not rock and
bog appeared to be the grass-covered detritus of an old quarry.
As land it was almost useless: it grazed a few head of cattle in
the summer; it provided us plentifully with rushes for thatching
our homestead or corn stacks and would have provided us liberally
with peat for fuel had the land laws of Ireland in those days been
framed for aught else than the exploitation of tenants by the
landlords. Not a turf dared we cut except at an extra rental which
would make the royalties once charged on English coal look like
petty pilfering compared with wholesale robbery.

My father clung – my brother still clings – to these worthless
acres for sentimental reasons. They were the place of origin of
one of the septs of the South Armagh Murphies, the Hughie
Mors, as my family is still named. There into a one-room cabin
my grandfather, Hughie Mor Murphy (*anglice*, Big Hugh Murphy),
had brought his bride, Sally Wan (fair-haired Sally), one of the
'Ballsmill Murphies', and, I have been told, the belle of South
Armagh in her youth. In that cabin were born Hugh's six children.
From money saved from relief work in the famine years; from

money earned as barge-tower on Ulster canals (it seems that on the Irish canals in the early days haulage was by men, not by horse); from his Herculean toil in English harvest fields Hughie had somehow managed to 'gather' the sixty pounds for the purchase of the farm in Carnally on which we of our generation were born. Hughie's strength and endurance have become a legend in the baronry of the Fews. I saw him when he was over eighty carry a five-hundred-weight sack of oats as if it were but a packet of groceries. The day before he died he walked the five miles to Tullyvallen Red Bog and from it walked home again just to see the place of his birth and to say goodbyes to such friends of his youth as still survived. I remember his coming into the kitchen in Carnally after that walk, his sitting down to his supper of stir-about, his shaking of his leonine head when the meal was over and his saying that it would be his last supper for he had heard the call of his people and would die the next day. And die next day he did at the age of ninety.

As I first remember us we were not poor as poverty was then measured in 'Carnally Rocks'. We had four or five cows, a good stock of young cattle, of pigs and sheep and sometimes two working horses. We had, inference of affluence, a servant girl. And there was 'dry money' in the house, that is, some reserve of cash surplus to immediate needs.

Though my father had saved some money from his English harvesting – he knew every inch of the Fens – this comparative wealth was largely due to my mother's 'fortune'. She had been one of a large family living on the side of the road by which my father passed to the second farm. On the maid looked the man; on the man looked the maid, and each, let their first-born say it, was good to look upon. I have heard neighbours say of them that on their 'bride's Sunday' they were the finest looking couple in 'the seven parishes'. Her people were accounted gentlefolk. Her father had inherited from an uncle much money as well as sixty acres of the best land in County Armagh. Brian Carragher was thus a gentleman by his position; doubly so if an indulgence in day-dreaming, in the reading of books and the arguing about Irish history and legend while the corn was going with the wind be qualities that go to the making of a gentleman. He nurtured a blind opposition to the marriage of any of his children: though he liked my father as one who could converse with him of the days when heroes walked the land, he would not have him for a son-in-law. The young couple then eloped. Brian then made the best of a bad job, gave them his blessing and, to his daughter, a 'fortune' of seventy pounds.

Despite all this we gradually sank to what was accepted as the inevitable role for all families in Carnally: poverty and debt while the children were growing up; a slow paying off of the debt when the children, grown up or half grown up, had become able to earn money. I recall the winter's day on which, the rent becoming due, my father would have to ask the landlord for time in which to make up the amount or borrow 7/6. From whom to borrow even that trifling sum? One might as well ask the devil for a chance of salvation as ask our landlord for time.

On such narrow margins did existences run in the rocks and bogs of South Armagh towards the close of the nineteenth century, but from what I have since learned I have no reason to suppose that they ran one whit more narrowly for us than existence ran for the working populations of the English and Scottish towns to which the Irish fled as soon as they were able. However, it was necessary that as soon as a child was able to do any work of any kind he or she should be 'aff to the stranger', that is, be hired to the richer farmers farther north in Tyrone or Down. For all that the people had a pathetic faith in the benefits to be derived from education or from 'schooling' as it was called. 'Schooling' might raise a lad to becoming a shop assistant in Belfast or Dublin, and to be a 'shop-boy' or a 'shop-girl' was esteemed somewhat better than being a mere hired hand on some Protestant's farm. So to school we went as soon as our little legs could carry us over the rough paths to Glassdrummond. There was no compulsory school attendance, but every child in our district of the parish of Crossmaglen or Upper Creggan, as it is more correctly named, was harried off to Michael McDonnell or his sister, who were the schoolmaster and schoolmistress in Glassdrummond. Before the children went to school, their parents taught the little things all they could so that they might start their schooling in the first, second or third 'books', as the standards were then called among us, not 'on the walls' as was said of those children who had to learn the alphabet and the reading of monosyllabic words from posters on the school walls.

My father took my education in hand when I was able to speak. I was then, I have often since been told, turned three, and by the age of six I was able to read very well, had advanced as far as proportion in arithmetic and could write letters for the neighbours to grown-up sons and daughters thanking the latter for the remission of sums of money to Carnally that would enable the parents to keep the roof over their heads.

I went into the third 'book' the day I first went to school. I remember it, sixty years ago, as if it were but yesterday. It was a wet Monday of June 1887. I was in charge of a neighbour's son. Tommy Jemmy Dhu, that is, putting our Irish nomenclature into English, Tommy, the son of Black Jemmy. The surname was Lavelle.

It was a noisy school. We were set our lessons and expected to learn them from books all purchased by ourselves even to the exercise books. We were deluged with various forms of homework, including sums and essays; and we were caned if we didn't do them, and caned if in the doing of them we displayed inaccuracy or lack of neatness. There was nobody to sympathise with us if we complained.

My first years in that school were mainly years of torture. But I fared better than I might while Tommy Lavelle was yet attending. Tommy, a big fellow of eighteen or so, ever laughing, would fight with generous abandon: there seemed to be a double measure of *élan* about his pugnacity if it were exercised on my account. No boy dared lay a hand on me while Tommy was about. But I had been going to Glassdrummond but for a few months when Tommy went off to Belfast to be a shop assistant. Tommy was the first of my lost shields of life.

Particularly did I suffer in my second winter in the school. Fear made me dull, my sums were ever wrong, I was always being caned, and I became a mark for the cruel wit of the bigger boys. I was the smallest child in the school. Some of the bigger lads in it were moustached men, fellows who, working in England or Scotland during the summer and returning home in the autumn, just came to school to while away the days when they could get no casual work on the small farms around Glassdrummond. They came to torture the smaller boys and to show off the tricks they had learned in their wanderings. The worst of them was a devil who boasted of the sobriquet he had acquired in Glasgow, 'Irish Pat O'Neill'. His strength was such that he could knock down a donkey with a blow of his fist. If he saw a donkey on the road, he made us all troop out of the school to witness his punching power. He would sometimes demonstrate it on the owner of the animal. He was closely followed in villainy of that kind by a fellow named 'Doctor' Griffin – I haven't the least idea why the 'Doctor' – a loosely built man, who, I should think, was over six foot tall and had an immense moustache. Michael McDonnell was not without courage, but, having but one arm, he was helpless before these bullies. I was still wearing petticoats. They would seize me, put me across their knees and indulge in some drum-beating practice on my little behind.

Dreading school, I took to staying out, lying at the side of hedges all the day. How I suffered when it rained! For a whole winter, rain or snow, I never set foot in the school.

By my fourth or fifth year in the school I had begun to like it. The big bullies had all left for good: I was, though small for my years, growing a bit myself. I had greatly improved in my lessons; so much so that I was often given classes of younger lads. I had an extraordinarily retentive memory, being able to rattle off all the answers to all the sums on all the cards, which McDonnell handed out to the boys of the senior standards for their homework. There was over a gross of such cards; six to each letter of the alphabet with six sums on each. Every summer I became the proud possessor of pockets full of buttons and marbles for supplying the answers to these sums. I guess I had a goodly measure of the brains of the 'Ballsmill Murphies', and the brains of the 'Ballsmill Murphies' had become synonymous with cleverness in South Armagh. Unfortunately, it seemed that they never knew how to turn their brain power to practical account, a characteristic that I, alas, shared to the full.

When I had turned twelve, I was, though still small for my age, accounted a 'tight lad', reckoned to be as 'far as the masters could put me'. So in the second stage of the sixth standard I was occasionally earning sixpence a day on other farms at such jobs as gathering potatoes, spreading manure or 'dropping seed'. I had had one or two chances of going off to be a shop-boy, but my father had turned them down. I was thus within measurable distance of achieving the second best ambition of a South Armagh country lad: going out for hiring. Once hired, I would be able to chew tobacco, drink beer, 'have my hoult' with the girls, for such things were the signs of manhood amongst us.

Then occurred something which postponed for twelve years such an assumption of the *toga virilla* [a white toga worn by fourteen-year-old Roman boys as a symbol of their manood].

2

That something was the distribution of prizes for an examination that had, at the instance of a curate enthusiastic for education, been held for all the boys and girls of the parish a few weeks before I left Glassdrummond School. The examination was for those in the first or second stages of the fifth and sixth standards and was, so to speak, on a handicap. As the only one in the parish in the second stage of the sixth standard, I had to forfeit fifteen per cent of my aggregate marks. I had taken the examination, but the excitement of having the hiring fair but a few weeks ahead of me had almost blotted out all interest in it for me. For a month I had been a farmer's boy when it was brought back to my mind by a special message that I was to attend in Crossmaglen School on the first Monday evening in May, 1894, for the distribution of prizes. Given twopence to spend, I went into the village school on the appointed evening, far more for the fun of spending the coppers than from any hopes that I would get a prize. I was barefooted and collarless. I sought the rear seats in the school and, as the rays of a kindly May sun filtered in on me through the windows, I fell asleep. I had been working since daylight.

At the jab of an elbow in my ribs I woke up. The parish priest was calling angrily for number 182. I was still sleep-dazed as my fingers went to my waistcoat pocket. In big black figures on the slip of crumpled paper I drew therefrom were these figures. There were hisses of 'Gwan up!' My emotions were those of complete bewilderment. It was only a call from Michael McDonnell at the head of the room that started me to movement. Collarless, barefooted and tousled of hair, I plopped up the hall in my patched corduroys. The angrily envious looks of the village boys, resplendently dressed in comparison with me, were fixed on me. 'Glassdrummond!' these lads barked at me. 'Wait till we get you outside!' They hated the boys from Glassdrummond, as for some time that school had been considered the best in the parish. It has, I learn with much satisfaction, in late years often been adjudged the best elementary school in Northern Ireland. Away back on that May evening of 1894 I stood as proof of its superiority over those immediately around it.

I received as my prize a large atlas of the world and a copy of Joyce's *History of Ireland*. I took them back to my place, and my childhood pal, Peter Gollogly, and I consulted how we might get them and ourselves out of the village in safety.

After the prize-giving we had music on the piano, an instrument that up till then I had thought to have only a mythical existence. Schoolmasters and schoolmistresses sang to us. The priests made speeches to us. Glowing things were said about my wonderful examination marks. It appeared that I could have had thirty per cent of my aggregate taken away and yet have won first place. Glassdrummond was on a high pedestal that night. The first prize for the girls of the parish had been won by one of its girls. Poor sharer of my childhood's glory! I learned the other day that she had just died of cancer. Always prone to floridity, Michael McDonnell's face above his bronze beard was almost on fire. Though a bit rough in his methods, he was a great teacher and had a passionate interest in teaching.

When I got home with the books, all question of my taking my stand on the hiring-fair, to which I should have gone in another five days with the prospect of working six months for some Protestant farmer for about 30/-, my food and a corner of the barn in which to sleep, was laid aside. My father decided I was to go back to school. Somewhere, he thought, the world should hold for a bright lad like me a position easier than slaving on a farm as a hired boy or 'hopping on the lug of a spade' in Carnally Rocks. As the news of my success spread about, the neighbours came in to offer me their rude congratulations and to have a look at the atlas and the history book. I found compliments very pleasant.

On the next Sunday I remained on at Glassdrummond chapel for Sunday School (catechism), not from any desire for the spread of religious knowledge but from the hope that by doing so I was putting myself in the way of receiving further compliments. I was sitting in front of ten younger little devils, putting them questions from the Maynooth catechism and listening to their monotonously choroused answers when the curate who had said Mass came along and sat down beside me.

'How would you like to go to college and be a priest?' he asked me.

He might as well have asked me how I would like to climb up into the night sky and pull down a star.

He explained that there were exhibitions to be won, two of as much as ten pounds a year each for two years, on an entrance examination, and expatiated on the great honour for myself and Glassdrummond School if I won them. Hitherto these exhibitions had gone to young fellows from towns in which there were advanced schools such an institutions run by the Christian Brothers, academics and special schools of that sort. Would I, bearing the banner of Glassdrummond, enter into competition with lads from such schools for these exhibitions? There would be further opportunities of even bigger awards. He'd explain the whole scheme to my father. Meanwhile, I'd have to go back to Glassdrummond School, learn algebra, Euclid and a few other things of which I had not as yet heard.

Well, the very next day I went back to Glassdrummond School. Jealousies soon broke out between me and the monitors (pupil teachers), both of them, though junior in school status to me, much bigger and older boys than I was. I thought myself the glory of the school and I would increase that glory if I passed the government examination for the second stage of the sixth standard. No boy from Glassdrummond had yet accomplished that feat. The monitors hid my books, and one day Michael McDonnell caned me for not knowing my lessons. My father gave me a hiding for losing my books. These injustices stirred me to fury, and, damning masters, monitors, exhibitions and colleges alike, I declared I would never again set foot in school.

In this revolt my father took an unexpected course with me. In charge of the landlord's cattle grazing on evicted farms in our vicinity was a retired schoolmaster, who, having commuted his pension, had, while the money lasted, been a very good customer of the local pubs. This man, John McCann, whose memory I still bless, would teach me the ordinary school subjects. Somewhat reluctantly I agreed to try this variation of the one-time Irish hedge-school.

If the day were fine, McCann and I lay out on a hillside. If it were wet, we sheltered in somebody's barn. He instilled into me an understanding of much that had so far been to me mostly memory work. He brought me books to read. It was strange to me that Shakespeare, Dryden, Pope and Byron should have written not merely the excerpts I had read in the school readers but whole volumes of poetry.

McCann's special subject was English, and what a grand teacher of it was that drunken old cowherd! He taught it well because he himself could use it beautifully. By his mastery of it he stirred me to an eagerness for progress. When half a century later I was trying to teach it, I had him in mind as my model. He could lose himself in it. Dream-enraptured, gazing at the purple mountains, Slieve Breac, Slieve Foy and Slieve Gullion, he would recite long passages of poetry or fling at me the coinages of his own mind, so grandly minted that my unattuned mind could not tell whether they were quotation or composition. And his reward for his teaching of me was a pound of butter and a can of buttermilk a week. Glad was he of that payment in kind, but I think he would have been even gladder of something more readily convertible into the drink for which his soul ached. Once my mother gave him a shilling as both butter and milk happened to be in low supply with her. That day he often took the coin from his pocket and spat on it. Each time he did so I could hear him murmur ecstatically, 'Six bottles of stout!' Guinness was then twopence a bottle.

Within a month peace was patched up between Michael McDonnell and myself. I returned to school, but spent my evenings with the cowherd.

I walked through the government examination. The inspector sent for me to congratulate me on my fine showing in it.

In the holidays that followed I went through the harvest tasks usual in Carnally for a lad who was 'rising thirteen'. I lifted corn and flax, pitched corn and hay, but every day a few hours were set aside for instruction from McCann. Indeed, as the weather got cooler and the cattle needed less herding, he'd come along to where I was working, walking up and down the corn swathe with me or the row of flax, teaching much orally.

August glided out in warmth and the pitching of corn onto cart or stack. September, misty of morn, often frosty and with days of chill, blustery rain, passed by. With its end the question of my future had to be transferred from the vague to the definite. There were conferences about it between the priests and my father. Our parish priest, being a member of the council that controlled the college entrance examinations, felt sure he would be able to have them fixed for a date that would mean my being under age for them. I, taking a chance on that – otherwise they would be held at a time which would just place me outside the age limit for them – was to go back to school and learn all I could. It would do me no harm. 'Learning,' said my father, with his usual sententiousness, 'is the only load that never skins the shoulders or makes the back sore.' I went back quite eager to explore the new fields of learning which were opening out to me.

Shock number one was soon to come to us. Hitherto my school books had cost a few coppers each: now we were to think in shillings about them. McDonnell obtained for me algebra and Euclid textbooks and a small book on English history. Five shillings the three came to. That was a sum that took some getting together in the early days of October before the corn was threshed and sold and the pigs killed and sold. My mother, tucking a squawking hen under each arm, trudged into Crossmaglen with them, sold them and so got the five bob.

It was long before I found any mental satisfaction in either algebra or Euclid. McCann had aroused in me a passion for understanding as distinct from merely remembering things. That winter was for me one of great mental strife. But McDonnell gave me great help in the grasping of coefficients and indices, of angles, triangles, and the other weird things across which I came in my studies so that by Easter 1895 I once again felt on top of the world.

By that time had come the news that the examination for the exhibitions would be held in August. This would just take me within the age limit. I was showing such progress in my new studies that it was generally accepted I would be successful. I ran about the Rocks clad in intellectual pride if not in much else. There had been another parish examination that year and invested with much more pomp than the one the previous year. To ensure that this time there would not be the slightest suspicion of favouritism the papers for it were set and were to be marked by a Dublin examiner. I, as the only boy or girl in the parish who had passed the second stage of the sixth standard, was this time to forfeit thirty per cent of my aggregate. The prize was to be a gold watch donated by our enthusiastic curate.

The examiner kept us on tenterhooks so long that we almost forgot all about the result. At last on a damp evening in July we were again assembled in the Crossmaglen School to hear the result. Barefooted as before, I again plopped up to receive the gold watch, the only one I have ever had.

It had a short life. My youngest brother, who had a curiosity about machinery and later on became for South Armagh something of an expert in it, set about it with a hammer and cold chisel to find out what made it tick.

The August days of 1895 sped by in whirls of excitement for us. Lists of clothing I was to have came from the college. One thing completely flummoxed us. I was to have two nightshirts. What was a nightshirt? Luckily a neighbouring woman who had once been a servant to a parish priest was able to enlighten us.

There came the day to which I had been looking forward with much excitement and some trepidation. It was the last day on which, bare-legged with my trousers rolled above my knees, I would skip over the Rocks, leap the Lurgan stream, steal vetches from the cornfields through which we passed or eat the succulent young swedes from some poor farmer's patch of root crops.

On the Sunday I was at Mass in Glassdrummond old chapel and gazed at by all because of my grandeur. At the end of the service the poor people clustered round me to say to me their goodbyes and to wish me good luck. The assistant teacher of the school, a Cork man, Paddy Galvin, slipped me half a crown as he shook my hand. Poor chap! On his salary of thirty pounds a year he can not have had many of them to spare. There were gifts of shillings and sixpences from others who could ill afford them.

On the Monday morning, August 25th, 1895, we were up at three, and by five my father and I were ready to set out on our journey to Armagh City. My tin trunk was locked and hoisted onto the farm cart, which had been specially washed for the occasion. In its shafts was our one mare, Fanny, prancing and tossing her proud head. Into the drawing of a plough or a cart about Carnally Rocks Fanny had brought something of the grace of the *haute école* of the circus.

On our way we called in to see my uncles and my aunts, the Carraghers of Drummill, two old bachelors and four old maids, all to live and die as slaves of the Irish land. My oldest uncle put a pound note in my hand, and that good deed he did every time I returned to the college after a vacation. 'Son,' he said to me one day as he gave me the money, 'yer head may be gettin' full iv laarnin', but there's one thing the books won't laarn ye,

15

an' that is how lonely the best road is if ye have nothin' in yer pocket.' Well, I have learnt that often enough.

The greater part of the road to the city was strange to me, and Fanny, fresh in from grass, had to be driven slowly. But the journey was enlivened for me by the tales from Irish legends my father told as Fanny clumped along. Now even there the tale of the Valley or the Black Pig and of The Bull's Tracks are just 'ould nonsense'. In the legends the Black Pig and the Bull were manifestations of the Devil, striving to oppose Saint Patrick's conversion of Ireland.

Arrived in the olden city, we had something to eat in a place that offered 'entertainment to man and beast' and then called on the president of the college, a very ascetic-looking old man. The bitter kindliness of his tongue I was to learn in the years immediately ahead of me. In years as yet far distant when I was an Australian officer strutting about London wearing on my shoulder the gilt 'A' that proclaimed me a genuine Anzac I was to hear that he, still teaching Classics, was still referring to me as the brightest boy he had ever steered through Homer.

Later in the evening my father and I carried my tin trunk up to the college. I was bidden goodbye, assured that there was a home for me to which I could return if I failed the examinations; but I know that failure would bring disgrace on the Ballsmill Murphies and would mean for me a life of slavery.

3

However, I did not fail. I got through one examination by a very commendable margin and through the other by a few marks. I thus had scholarships each of which was worth ten pounds a year and tenable for two years. So, I had gained twenty pounds a year towards the annual college fee of thirty pounds. The purchase of books would be quite an expense. For my upkeep at the college there would have to be found a further fifteen pounds yearly, and this was an immense sum to be scraped from eight acres of Carnally Rocks.

But there were held out to me visions of other examinations by which in the coming years these charges might be met. When my present scholarships had run out, there was a further one to be won of twenty pounds a year for three years. The mysteries of the old Irish Intermediate System of Education with its yearly exhibitions varying in value according to the grades in which they were secured were explained to me. Some of these exhibitions were worth thirty pounds a year. It was made to appear to me that had I the brains and application, I might yet be helping my people instead of being a burden to them. Anyhow, my father decided I should stay on at the college; somehow or another, he would scrape up the extra money.

A fortnight was to elapse before the general body of the boys returned to the college at the end of the normal vacation. Life in that fortnight, apart from some difficulty in learning the correct way to use a handkerchief, the use of the rather crude sanitation of the college and the proper way of eating with knife and fork (in Carnally we had never bothered about such matters), was simple enough. I was intensely lonely, though the college priests tried to cheer me up and interest me in various games and establish friendships between me and a few other lads who had remained on in the college after the examinations. But these lads were endlessly playing handball, about which I as yet know nothing, and I liked to moon about by myself, ever hoping that my father, Fanny and the farm cart would come and take me back to the Rocks.

When at the end of the vacation the general crowd of students returned, life seemed to got very complicated. There was no more time for mooning and dreaming. All day there was a frantic rushing about from room to room when a bell rang, and nobody thought it worth while to point out to me where I should rush or why I should rush. Meals, too, were a scramble, in which the 'cub' was apt to fare badly though there was at each table a refectory prefect who was supposed to see that the plain and not over-abundant food got fairly shared out. In the evenings we were herded into a big study hall in which we prepared our work for the following day. Still, a little display of kindness from the dean, a golden-haired giant of a priest, reconciled me to the place at least a little bit. I soon established some reputation as a 'cub' with an extraordinarily retentive memory for the irregularities of Greek and Latin declensions and conjugations. It was thought I would do very well at the Christmas College examinations at the end of my first term.

I didn't. I was so eager to do well that I accepted help from a senior boy during the Greek test, was caught, severely caned and deprived of all my marks. I was held up as a thoroughly bad example to the whole college.

This 'cogging' incident brought me much grief, mental and physical. The kindly and almost fatherly interest with which I had been treated in the first term thenceforward gave way to harshness from all the staff. This drove me to sulkiness and lack of interest in all things scholastic. Daily I figured in the punishment queue. I thought it a noble thing to affect idleness, but towards the end of the Easter term I worked rather seriously and, though at the Intermediate examinations in 1896 I did not get an exhibition, I had the highest marks of my grade in the college and got some little distinction in the way of special book prizes.

My second year was very much like my first. I absorbed a lot of punishment because of unfavourable reports about me from the prefects, again worked hard as summer was coming along and again missed the coveted Intermediate exhibition, having to be content with another book prize. The exhibitions of the college which I had won two years before were now at an end, but I managed to secure the Senior college one of twenty pounds a year.

I spent my summer vacations herding cows, lifting or tying hay and doing other odds and ends of work on our rocky farm. There were a couple of other 'collegers' from our district. But they were the sons of shopkeepers, had bicycles and money to spend. All I could do was to moon about the Rocks, noting the cloud-cast shadows flit over the ripening crops and sweep in wondrous play of light and shade up the slopes of Slieve Gullion and, taking, it seemed to me, pieces of my young soul with them, vanish into the accumulated mysteries beyond the mountain-rimmed horizon. I was generally glad when the day came for my return to the college.

In the beginning of my third year there I got what I considered a most unjust caning along with some other forms of punishment, such as the loss of some trivial prefectships in dormitories and at a refectory table. This unmerited degradation led me to the formation of a resolve that in conduct and application to study I would make of myself the model boy of the place. I think I succeeded. Fifty years afterwards old priests who had been in my class were quoting me to my own sons as an example of hard work that was unequalled in the Armagh of their and my day.

Somewhere I had read the definition of genius attributed to Carlyle: 'an infinite capacity for taking pains'. There was more than mere vanity in my awareness that I had ability in considerable measure. With this ability I would now ally the taking of pains.

I burnt all my translations of the set Greek, Latin and French texts, working with no help but my dictionaries and grammars and doing other things that were always being recommended to us.

The consequence of this change of method was that, though I often fell behind in the volume of work done, there were very favourable comments on the quality of what I did. Thus encouraged, I put my nose still closer to the grindstone. I had the satisfaction of having young men who had been trying for two years to pass the final college examination come to me for assistance. In the summer of that third year I had come first in the college tests in every subject but French, and in the autumn when the results of the middle-grade Intermediate examination were published my name was pages ahead of that of any other boy in the grade from the college. I had got a special book prize and a small special cash prize, but the exhibition had again been missed by no more than about twenty marks. Thus, there was still a large yearly sum to be found for me from the Rocks, and by this time my brother and two of my sisters had taken their stands on the child slave market of the hiring-fairs to contribute their little earnings towards the finding of it.

In the last year of mine at the college I should normally have been looking forward to leaving it for Maynooth, the Irish National Ecclesiastical Seminary for the final training for the priesthood. I had already decided that there would be no Maynooth for me. I would join the religious order whose priests were teaching in the college, I had read and been enthralled by the account of the life of their founder. Part of the work of the priests of the order lay in teaching, and it was this part that appealed to me, and what most appealed to me was the long years I imagined I would spend in study of the Classics to fit myself for that teaching. The announcement of my intention to join a religious order instead of going through Maynooth to the secular priesthood was a great disappointment to my poor father and mother, and to a certain extent to the priests of my native parish. They suspected quite rightly that what moved me to the religious life was the poverty of my people, and they offered to foot all my expenses right through Maynooth. In these arguments my mother was the first to take my part, and did so for the reason that no Ballsmill Murphy could ever be led or guided from a course determined upon.

In that last year of mine at the diocesan college I worked more eagerly than ever with my eyes on two ambitions: to get an Intermediate exhibition and to win the gold medal for Classics given by the Intermediate Board to the boy who in Latin and Greek got the highest marks in the senior-grade examination. Though Michael Carrigy rarely praised a student, he would go so far as to admit that Peter Murphy saved himself from utter disgrace in his English and was, I learned, telling the other priests, who in turn told me, that I had an extraordinary flair for the Classics. He approved of my intent to join his order and encouraged me by saying that in teaching I should prove of great service to it. At the same time he warned me of the difficulties that lay ahead of me during the two years' novitiate on my entrance into it. I was often being warned of these difficulties, but I was never one to look before leaping.

Soon after Easter in that last year I had a letter from my mother informing me that my father was very ill from double pneumonia resulting from a bad wetting he had while coming home from our distant farm. My brother had been called home from his place of servitude to work as well as a lad of fourteen could be expected to work our rocky farm in Carnally. There was but one way in which I could help in this deplorable situation; that was to leave the college, give up all notion of the priesthood, religious or secular, and go out to work as a hired labourer. I offered to do so, but the offer was rejected. I was to stay on in the college. The few pounds needed to meet the balance of my last year's fees would be found somehow, I was assured. A 'spoilt priest' would be a greater misfortune than poverty.

In the middle of June I got word that my father was somewhat better; the doctor thought there was a chance of his pulling through. At the end of the month I was interviewed by the Provincial of the order. He accepted me as a postulant for admission to it, informed me that he would later on communicate with me on where I was to enter on that admission, what clothes I was to have with me and such mundane trifles. When told of the desperate poverty at home, he took it on himself to pay what fees were still due for me to the college. As I knelt for his blessing at the end of the interview, I felt that the world was not wholly an unkindly place.

There were still a few days left of the Intermediate examinations. I gave myself up with a renewed intensity to those that remained in the hope that I might secure an exhibition or the gold medal. I got neither. I missed the medal by a few marks, the exhibition by about twenty. I had merely the empty satisfaction of taking top place of the senior entrants from all over Ireland in Greek, getting eleven hundred marks out of twelve hundred.

On that last summer holiday from Armagh I found my father as one who had returned from the shadow. He was able to sit up a little, but small was the comfort in a Carnally farmhouse for one who required ease and nursing. There was a hard wooden chair before a smoky slag fire. Yet in a few weeks he was able to totter about for a few hours daily. Just as things seemed on the way to being all right with him, he most unexpectedly got a relapse, and had to take to the bed from which he never again rose.

As August drew to a close, he was nigh to death. From the Provincial of the order I had received instructions that, having provided myself with a black suit in which I was to figure a Chesterfield coat (I had not the slightest notion what sort of a garment that was) and a tall silk hat, I was to report at the central novitiate on September 3rd. But black cloth for clerical wear, Chesterfield coats, silk hats were beyond the clothing and tailoring resources of Crossmaglen. An aunt of mine who had some money of her own very generously and with very good intent bought me a brown suit. That with the black trilby I had had as a *de rigeur* article of garb in the diocesan college would have to serve.

On the last Tuesday of that August my father died and on the first of September he was buried in the new graveyard at Glassdrummond, the first of the Ballsmill Murphies to be buried elsewhere than in 'generous, greedy Creggan' of the Gaelic poets, but the story of Creggan, however inviting for the telling, is one for the archaeologists.

Next day, as my mother and brother refused to hear of my staying at home to help them in their struggle, I set out for the novitiate. Sometime that evening I reached it in one of the southern suburbs of Dublin. I was weary from lack of rest and tearful because of the kindness with which I was received. I had a meal with the community, walked for an hour in a lovely fruit garden, went to bed in a big, bright room and slept for fourteen hours.

4

I soon began to realise that my life in the novitiate would not be in the least the sort of life I had imagined it would be. Had I known any art of fending for myself or had I had the courage to face the hearts I would break by going home, I would almost instantly have left it.

There was, it was explained to me by a student of the place appointed to expound the life of the novitiate to myself and four other newly arrived postulants while we walked the fruit garden during our four days of silent 'retreat' before our formal acceptance as 'postulants', no study for me for the next two years. The dictionaries, grammars and textbooks, which I had taken along with me to be my consolation, would all be taken away from me and packed in a storage loft. In their place I would have only 'spiritual' books. And those mainly in English. The only Latin book I would have would be a copy of the Catechism of the Council of Trent, which I found to be a very dog-Latin compilation. After some time as a very special favour I was given permission to read the New Testament in Greek. The Evangelists may have been divinely inspired, but not as Hellenists.

The next two years were to be spent in learning to be humble, mortified and obedient. My days were to be spent in a series of spiritual and corporal exercises designed to destroy conceit, pride and self-will. No doing what I liked to do, but doing what I disliked doing, and the more I disliked it the better for my soul. And doing things at the times set out for the doing of them. Every half-hour from 6.30 a.m. till 9.30 p.m. a bell would ring. At its very first tingle one was to stop whatever one had been doing and dash off to start something else. Sometimes that was a relief, sometimes not. The least failure to comply with the routine was likely to earn an offender humiliating penances such as scrubbing a lavatory or doing with one's hands some gardening task that was usually done with a spade.

Perhaps two years of this discipline might have broken down my moodiness, my introspection and my obstinacy. Probably to my undoing I had no more than a few months of it in its strictest application. After a few weeks I fell sick and spent over a month in bed. The doctor called in to vet me said there was nothing more serious the matter than that I had been overworked and undernourished. Given a variety of tonics to build me up, I joined once more in the 'community' life and was beginning to find it fairly tolerable when, in the early months of 1900, such community life was brought to a standstill for close on three months by an outbreak of influenza that put all inmates of the monastery – priests, students, novices and lay brothers alike – on the horizontal.

When after Easter the normal general routine was re-established, I was exempted from a number of the practices of the novitiate in order that I might translate from Latin a volume containing the religious counsels of the order's founder and pious recommendations from its Superiors-General or general councils. This book was read out to the assembled community at each annual retreat. The Spiritual Director in my days in the novitiate, thinking it odd that a book like it should be read to men in a language which three in five of the hearers wouldn't understand, obtained the permission of the Irish Council of the order for its translation. He had me approved of as the translator. I fear his thus setting me apart as one more gifted than the other young fellows about me was not very good for my mean soul. For three or four annual retreats I heard my translation being read out to the community. The intention, I was told, was one day to have it printed and circulated to all the English-speaking houses of the order. Whether that has been done I don't know: I like to think it has.

Life for the novices was not vastly different from that for other sections of the community or as I might call it, though not wholly correctly, the monastery. The other sections were the students, young men who, having completed their novitiate, had taken the simple vows of poverty, chastity and obedience and so were *de jure* members of the order, engaged in theological study for the priesthood. There were a number of priests engaged in teaching various sacred subjects or in administration of the order, and lastly there were some six or seven lay brothers, who did the menial work of the monastery. They all, though there were occasional grumbles, accepted in a spirit of general cheerfulness the life in community. It was not a very hard life. The food was good and plentiful and there was for us younger folk and for the older ones who cared to join in with us a reasonable amount of recreation: cricket, tennis, football, handball according to the season. Every Wednesday was a free day. We could go swimming to a famous bathing place mentioned in one of the novels of L.A.G. Strong, a place that to me always seemed to refute the statement one so often hears, that the Irish will quarrel over anything. There in that bathing place Protestant and Catholic, priest and parson got along in complete amity. Some of us swam in the open sea all the year round.

On our free day, we could choose between swimming and going for a walk in pairs to some selected spot in the Dublin or Wicklow mountains. Sharing in the communal games and recreations was compulsory unless exempted from them under medical advice. Generally the sharing in them was quite pleasant for the confrères were good humoured and very kindly. It was having to share with them when I found something more interesting, such as reading some book I had come across in my student years, that I, ever the fifth wheel on the waggon, found irritating.

We had many feast days throughout the year. On these days not merely was the routine relaxed, but there was real feasting of the spirit and the body. The impressive ceremonies of the Church for such festivals were performed in our little chapel with full ritual: there was a community dinner which would have rejoiced the heart of an English housewife in these days; after the dinner there was a little port wine for those who liked it and lots of fun for everybody, as anybody who could play, sing, recite, even tell a story, contributed to the entertainment of his brethren.

We had the usual holiday periods of Christmas, Easter and midsummer, during which the rigour of the rule was greatly relaxed. Every day in these periods was a free day, though not all were feast days. A month of the summer holiday period would be spent at a large lay college of the order to the north of Dublin. To that month at Knockcaisleann, as I here name the place, we all looked forward. While we were in it, we missed the sea bathing, the wide golden strands on the south side of Dublin Bay, the rambles up the mountains, but as compensation we had the fine covered swimming bath of the college, in which young fellows who had taken to the water almost as a second medium of existence could disport themselves. Facilities for other sports were vastly better than in the monastery. Here were cricket pitches and tennis courts onto which no cow was ever allowed to wander. There were two ball alleys, but our liking for that fine Irish game was beginning to lessen. Inside the college there were splendid billiard tables, and as we trotted round them we might delude ourselves that one day we might become rivals to John Roberts, then the king of the billiard world. There were grand pianos for those with a taste for music; there were libraries full of secular books for those who liked to read. There I made the acquaintance of Stevenson and George Eliot, sitting up sometimes all night to find out what had become of Jim Hawkins and Squire Trelawney or to weep when Tom and Maggie Tulliver were drowned as the ruins of Dorlcote Mill swept down on their boat. It might have been better for my romantic, yet mean, nature if my acquaintance with these tales had been postponed to later years. They and other like works were revealing to me that I had not known the world on which I had so lightly turned my back; that there were in it emotions I had not experienced and was now cut off from experiencing.

The college buildings ever breathed into me the atmosphere of their romantic situation. One approached their outer gates up a gentle slope of the great Dublin park; from these gates a winding drive led down to a mass of buildings filling an opening between two conical hills. That on the east was by legend linked with Cuchulain, Finn and his Red Branch Knights. On the western one were the ruins of a Norman castle, around which the Normans of the Pale and the Irishry from the hills had freely shed one another's blood. The slopes of that hill had been laid out in flower gardens that at points had been extended even between the crumbling walls. I loved to walk in them on dewy mornings when the air was perfumed by the scents of roses, the dew drops on the leaves were an infinitude of pearls and the grass in the long dried-up castle moat sparkled with innumerable diamonds. I would have my strolls here at eve, when the sunset was flaming the sky over the great central plain at the back of the college with a tangle of lakes of blue with what seemed to me wool-fleeced lands of mystery.

After our month in that college we would return to the monastery to find life in it a trifle dull, the seaside ramble and the walks up the mountains somewhat of a *pis aller* [last resort]; and the closure of the summer holiday by eight days of silent retreat was justified on more than spiritual grounds by its bringing of us back to a realisation that life was just one 'damned thing after another'. In a few weeks we would settle down to the humdrum of our monastic existence.

And, indeed, life in the monastery was not, except for a never-satisfied chap like myself, too much of a burden. In its own way the monastery had scenic attractions just as great as those of Knockcaisleann. The core of its buildings was an old mansion which those who some sixty years before had established the Irish branch of the order had made its headquarters in Ireland. Alongside this old building had been constructed a three-storey building, which, though not completed in my time, was yet a gracious thing in design. Around the buildings stretched some twenty or thirty acres of farm lands, through which hurtled a mountain stream flowing through a little lake in the grounds. The land was rich and well wooded: on it we had our tennis courts, our cricket pitch, our football pitch. Gravelled paths wound about the lake, and part of our recreation was to keep these paths in good order. Participation in games was compulsory unless one was sick. I don't suppose our cricket or football ever rose much above the level of that displayed by youngsters on corners of London commons, but our games were marked by good humour and the higher qualities of sportsmanship. And they were played in a glorious setting. On the horizon was the semicircle of the purple mountains; between us and them lay the Dublin plain so thick with trees that an imagination less prone to weaving than was mine could imagine we were gazing on the primeval forest.

Most of the land was excellently farmed. The monastery was self-supporting as regards vegetables, fruit, milk, butter and eggs. In the farming we played no part. That was carried on by hired laymen. The cropping was attended to by a James O'Hagan, so stolid and so slow of movement that as he trudged behind his horses he looked like a lump of animated earth. Another layman, Malachy Moran, aged, bearded and bent with toil, looked after the cows and hens. With them was Ben Curran, the gardener, much younger and much more sprightly than either O'Hagan or Moran, remotely affable as he lorded it over his greenhouses, potting sheds, vegetable and fruit gardens and flower-beds. Ben and the Father Provincial had almost opposite points of view about vegetables and flowers. The old priest rather despised flowers as things that served no useful end, and was always urging Ben to a greater production of vegetables instead of spending so much of his time on his flowers. Vegetables were things to which Ben attended somewhat unwillingly. With Ben the beautiful was the useful, and a bed of multicoloured asters had more worth in his eyes than all the cauliflowers or sprouts ever grown.

As I have mentioned, there was still plenty of manual work for students and novices to do in connection with the paths and rockeries in the grounds. To each of us was allotted a section of them to be kept in order. This work was done in the morning recreation periods, during which talking was not permitted. So after breakfast we went to the tool sheds, took from them hoes, rakes, shears, lawnmowers, and what else was needed for our work. But so long as one's section was in reasonably good order, there was no necessity to be ever toiling at it. If one liked, one might go to the ambulatory, a long, covered shed, in which we walked in bad weather. In it were rings, parallel bars and much other such equipment. There one could engage in almost any gymnastic practice. Some of the students and novices, those who had been trained in the semi-public schools round Dublin, were quite proficient gymnasts. *Mens sana in corpore sano* [a healthy mind in a healthy body] was the ideal at which the monastery aimed. One was held to be just as important as the other.

As a result of this ideal I and a couple of other young lads in the novitiate – hobbledehoys, undersized and round shouldered like myself – were told by the Director of Novices that we would have to undergo a course of physical training. For this training we were put under the care of a senior novice, a Cork man, at whose feats on rings and bars we had often stared open-mouthed. For half an hour a day he put us through a severe course of Sandow's exercises, and whether it was due to a late development of physical powers characteristic of the Ballsmill Murphies or to the training – I suspect the latter played a part – I blossomed forth in my early twenties as a young chap of much strength and agility, and a bodily carriage that would have done credit to a guardsman.

I kept up the exercises for several years as a discipline for mind as well as for body. I learned from an American priest in Rome that the exercises could be even more beneficially performed without any equipment such as developers and dumb-bells. This young priest expounded to me the rudiments at least of thought control over muscle. I infer that some such system under a fancy name is now widely advertised as a means of turning C3s into

A1s. From my own experience of it I would say that it goes a long way in that direction.

So, as I have outlined it, was our living; on the whole not too hard, and even I after a time in the community settled down to a measure of contentment with the life. I was not exactly a shining example of cheerful acceptance of the many little irritations such a community life imposes on human nature. Perhaps had my novitiate run its normal course, I might have blossomed out as a passable imitation of a monk.

The biggest interruption to my novitiate came soon after the start of my second year in it. The hitherto unprecedented step was taken of starting five or six of us second-year novices on our philosophical studies. For these studies we were exempted almost wholly from the general exercises of the novitiate. This advancement of us into serious study long before the usual time for it was due to an increasing demands for priests of the order to cope with extensions of its work in the missionary and educational fields and to make up for the retirement of several of its older priests from their spheres of duty.

The philosophy we studied was, of course, scholastic, which, many of my modern-minded friends assure me, does not deserve the name of philosophy. However, as I have an equally contemptuous view of their arguments built up on assumptions and probabilities, honours in contempt are about level. And, whatever be the merits or demerits of the scholastic system *per se*, we were fortunate in that we had as our lecturer in it the lantern-jawed Father Pat O'Hagan, who had a strange faculty of always getting the mind to work. Whether he esteemed himself fortunate in having us as his students was another matter. In his early life he had been Professor of Philosophy in an Irish college on the Continent, and had in his late thirties been sent out on missionary work, from which he had been recalled to deal with us. He made no secret of his longing to be delivered from us and be back with the savages, and sometimes when his tongue was too raspish we wished we were. Four of the little bunch had had their Humanities in the large schools around Dublin, had matriculated and taken their Intermediates, then called First Arts and Second Arts, under the old Royal University of Ireland. It was decided that these four should have a shot at the University's BA Honours examination. It was here I was forced to realise that something had been missing in my preliminary education which would ever leave me out in the cold. At the end of the course these four could write BA after their names: although in Pat O'Hagan's opinion I knew more about philosophy, scholastic and modern, than the four put together. I was still plain Peter Murphy. How much easier that BA would have made my struggle in my fifties and sixties when I was trying desperately to dodge starvation by winning through to a position in the educational service of the London County Council.

However, I could not foresee the evils of thirty years ahead. Soon after the conclusion of the philosophy course I was due to take my vows as a member of the order. The taking of them was put off for several months. The Spiritual Director did not think that my individuality and impetuosity of temperament had been sufficiently toned down for me to take them. He declined to shoulder the responsibility of letting me take them and referred the matter to the Father Provincial, who at length assented rather doubtfully. I was more than a bit doubtful myself as to the wisdom of taking the vows, but it was the easier thing to do. I dreaded, knowing myself to be 'childish-foolish', going out into the world to fend for myself and facing the obloquy that would be attached to me as a 'spoilt priest'.

5

I took the vows, adverting that they were but simple vows, dispensable by the Superior-General, and as an established member of the community, 'both feet in' as we used to phrase it, started on my theology course in the autumn of 1902 as I was nearing my twenty-first birthday. Hopes ran high among the intellectually ambitious of us, and I was far from being the least so, for word had gone forth that each year the two looked upon as most likely to win through to doctorates in the sacred science itself and in the kindred sciences of scholastic philosophy and canon law would be sent to Rome to study at the ecclesiastical universities in that city. That autumn went my great friend P.P. and another student, and it was being hinted that in a year or two I was to follow them to the Eternal City.

I think I soon began to shine in our theology classes. That was not altogether because of knowledge of theology, but because they were conducted in Latin. Owing to that I had wide scope for the display of my vanity or concealing my ignorance beneath loquacity. Not for me was the bog-Latin of the textbooks or the still boggier Latin of the professors and my fellow students. I delighted in bringing wrinkles of perplexity to their foreheads by the employment of strictly classical usages. That was not wholly affectation. I know the language and I loved it. And one of the things that as a novice I should not have been doing was going about with a pocket edition of Cicero in my soutane; and when no doubt I should have been reading Thomas à Kempis, Rodriguez, Faber and other exponents of the life spiritual I was often reading Cicero's praise of himself or his wordy dissertations on other things. I had accustomed myself to think directly in the language.

So, I often used my fluency in Latin to cloak my want of knowledge of the question put me. One of the professors, a young priest from Royal Meath, once dealt rather severely with that dodge. 'Mr Murphy,' he interrupted me, 'you can just tell me in plain English what you don't know about the question.'

I cannot recall that I took very keenly to either of the branches of theology, dogmatic or moral, but as it was only through them I could hope to set my feet on the road to Rome I took care to know enough about them to shine at the half-yearly tests, which were more than a little forbidding as we went in singly to the examination room and had to face the order's recognised theological experts. Fate was very kind to me in the tests of the summer of 1903. All questions put to me were on points of which I had made a very keen study. My examiner was a remarkably softly voiced, elderly priest, acknowledged as one of the best theologians in Ireland. Praise was rarely given, but I got several '*optimes!*' from him. July of that summer found me by common report as due to start in September for a three-year stay in Rome. I was disappointed when I was not officially notified I was going, but this disappointment was assuaged by other interests I had created for myself. The difficulty was that I was ever creating interests for myself. Some of them were manual; some of them had to do with supplementary studies. The thing for a good monk was to plod quietly along the way marked out for him. I was always divagating quite a bit on schemes of my own and pursuing them with a rather burning zeal.

For instance, when another student put it into my head that it would be a fine thing to make a canoe for our lake out of the trunk of one of the many elms that had been blown down in a great storm the previous winter, I set about doing so, devoting for many months all my recreation time to this perfectly unnecessary task. I succeeded, but was it hard work? About the hardest I have ever done. A new Spiritual Director issued me my first warning about overdoing things. 'You see,' he advised, 'you lack all sense of discretion and of value. What will be the good of it? We have managed for sixty years without a boat. If we hadn't one for another sixty years, nobody would take much hurt. You go at everything like a bull at a gate. You'll just knock yourself up, and what then?'

I did knock myself up, but through an accident of getting a hand caught between a swinging door and its jamb on a very gusty morning. The doctor, who had in his earlier ministrations to me given me but few years to live, patched the hand up and told me that I was as strong as two horses. In my injured state I was given a nice single room, very kind attention by the brother in charge of the infirmary and heaps of secular literature to read. For the first few days of his coming to me the doctor spoke of the necessity for amputation of the arm, but I was as well as ever in a couple of months and was back making improvements to my canoe. I was studying just then Gaelic as these were the opening years of the Irish Revival, Italian with my eye on Rome, and Spanish for some reason I cannot now recall. Probably the only reason for it was to be doing something different from others.

Soon after my return to the normal routine of the community I began to suffer from violent headaches and a general lassitude out of which I had always to be spurring myself. I could not bring myself to imagine that I should suffer from the nervous breakdowns then becoming rather frequent among the student section of the community. I am afraid we regarded such breakdowns rather uncharitably, calling them 'tired heads'. Late in May, 1904, I became one of the 'tired heads'. As I was one day orating in my best Ciceronian manner, my fellow students, desks, professor, shelves lined with huge tomes on theology went into one vast blur, and I pitched headlong to the floor.

The doctor, whom, I think, I had somewhat disappointed by my denying him a valid reason for amputating my hand, seemed pleased to have me on his hands again. He had warned me to take things more quietly; so now he could chuckle at me, 'I told you so.' He laid down a diet and a timetable for me, prescribed various treatments, the administration of which kept the brother in charge of the infirmary, rest his soul, pretty busy, ordered the cessation of all study of any kind: all manual work was to stop, so was all exercise except that of the most gentle kind. And no exercise had been worthwhile for me unless it had been rather vigorous. I was just to stroll about the grounds, gaze on the green grass, watch the sunbeams dance on the little lake.

A month of this produced no beneficial result whatever. The doctor then advised that his last-hope remedy should be tried. That was to send the sufferer to his home so that he could have a complete change of surroundings. I was rather delighted when he won the consent of the Superior to this remedy, forgetting that I had not much of a home to go to.

When I got to Carnally Rocks, I found that my mother, brother, and youngest sister, who were all of the family now left in the cabin, had at times great difficulty in providing enough food for themselves. All the others, a younger brother and three sisters, were hired to help to pay off the debt accumulated by my four years in the diocesan college. Staying in the Rocks was out of the question. I at first went to reside with the uncle who during my terms at Armagh had been so generous to me in the matter of pocket money.

What I should have done was to go straight back to the community, gaze on the grass and hear the lake water lapping with low sounds by its shore. Unluckily for me I discovered I had some relatives in watering villages around Dundalk Bay. They had not much interested themselves in me while I had been a half-hungry, undersized youth struggling with the Classics. Now that I was a well-set-up young man of twenty-three they made much of me, quarrelling with one another as to which bunch of them I should stay with. They were all fairly comfortably off, having pubs, hotels and big boarding houses. I elected to stay with one set of them who had a brother booked for death through consumption and spent the better part of three months with them. During these three months I learned many things, such as how to ride a bicycle, how to sail a small boat and how to smoke cigarettes. I learned also that, if such a term can be applied to a male, I had more than a share of sex appeal. Anyhow my clerical garb – I should have changed into lay attire but had not the money to buy a suit of clothes – did not prevent one of these relatives from bursting out into an impassioned declaration of her love for me while I was, perhaps not very discreetly, expressing my sympathy with her on the death of her brother.

Again I should have fled back to the community. I stayed on with them and soon began to entertain the idea of love as an agreeable, but impossible dream. We got not beyond words, but we gave an opportunity for scandal that, I later found, was fully taken advantage of. There was a certain amount of wild, wet kissing, and a vague assent that if I could get a dispensation from my vows and a dispensation from the impediment of consanguinity, we would one day get married. When I did return to the community one wild wet night in October, 1904, I think, if I had yet learned to think clearly, there was not within me much notion of going on to the priesthood. That night happened to be my twenty-third birthday. (On my twenty-fourth, I stepped ashore in Cape Town and had all South Africa in front of me in which, as a layman, to find my first job. But that is to come.) The headaches returned as soon as I got back to monastic life. The doctor put me back on his 'dolce far niente' treatment [restitution through pleasant idleness]. That did not improve matters and he again advised a complete change of scene. I, as far as obedience allowed me to struggle, struggled that this change of scene should be the same as it had been during the summer, the Mourne Mountains and Dundalk Bay, but I found myself ordered to Rome with the proviso that after a couple of months of rest in the international house there I should start serious study again with a view to getting a couple of ecclesiastical degrees.

Getting to Rome was quite an adventure for one so little versed in travel as I. It was managed by the aid of Thos. Cook. After some slight misadventures I reached the Eternal City and handed myself over to my friend P.P. to be looked after by him as my Guardian Angel.

I just did nothing for these couple of months except stroll about the streets of Rome and make friends with the other inhabitants of the *casa internationale*. I was enrolled at one of its several Catholic universities and attended lectures in one of its great halls, occupying a seat in the remotest corner into which I could squeeze. That was among a group of quite Godly but much expectorating Portuguese.

My 'tired head' continued. There was no doctor to bother me with his recommendations. I spent whole nights awake listening distractedly to the tread of the *Carabiniero* who walked with measured and noisy step up and down our street or listening to the raucous gaiety from an all-night *trattoria* on the opposite side of the thoroughfare.

P.P., the other Irishman in the international house, studying very hard for his third doctorate, had so far been leaving me very much to my own devices, but early in the new year we went into a huddle as to what was now to be done. Attempts by me to secure doctorates were out of practical discussion, and at first it seemed to me a question of my returning to the Irish province of the order as a complete failure. But the discussion went deeper than that. That merry sprig of the Kerry dancers wheedled me into a revelation to him of what had transpired the previous summer, and he, master of himself and born to mastery of others, put the matter on the basis of whether or not I had a real vocation to the priesthood. The rule of the game as we had been taught to play it, was that now I should obtain the view of an eminent spiritual adviser as to my reverting to a layman and seeking a dispensation from my vows. He would have to be an English-speaking priest, for though by this time I was beginning to speak both Italian and French fairly fluently, I was far from being able to put my problem clearly and openly before a priest of either nationality.

I had become accustomed to going for my weekly confession to the rector of the Irish Franciscan house in Rome, a man famous then and more so later on for his learning in sacred studies and full, as we Irish like our priests to be, of the Grace of God and of human nature. He retained much of his native brogue and would address me as 'My son', and sometimes he would use the even sweeter Gaelic term 'Alanna' (my child).

'Alanna,' said he to me one evening when he had given me absolution and his blessing, 'what's troublin ye? You're not happy. What's the cause of that? Don't be afraid to tell me. And don't worry about time. Sure it was given us to spend, and mebbe we couldn't spend it better.'

Kneeling before him in the dim confessional of the weirdly shadowy church as a lay brother padded through it, lighting the lamps, I told him all.

'Now then, Alanna,' said he, when he had heard me through to the end, 'let the pair of us say a wee prayer to God for guidance. We're just a couple of His creatures groping in the dark, but we mean to do what's right, and He'll help us by His grace and light.

'Alanna mo cree [child of my heart] not only are you free to seek a dispensation from your vows, but I think you are bound to do so. But I suppose you are afraid to do that. You have been told that if you go out into the world, you'll be damned. I know that much. Now don't be a bit afraid. The world isn't altogether the wicked place that religious priests make it out to be. There's a great deal of wickedness and sin in it, of course, but there's a lot of good in it as well. Of course, there's a lot of temptation in it, but there's a lot of temptation in a monastery too, and it's worse there if it's yielded to. Remember God's good to us, and we have the sacraments and the Holy Mass. You may live a good Christian life outside a monastery as well as inside it; a better one, perhaps. God bless you, son: God and his Holy mother be always with you.

'Now you'll have to be making some kind of living for yourself. I am afraid you'll find that hard. You see, brought up as you have been brought up, there's nothing the world wants that you are especially qualified to do. The only thing I can think of for you is teaching. Our order has a couple of lay colleges in Ireland and has a couple of lay teachers in them. By what you've told me about yourself you'd be just the man for such post. I'll write tonight to the president of these colleges. I'll give you the addresses and as soon as you get back to Ireland lose no time in writing to them yourself.'

The next thing to do was to write to the Irish Provincial notifying him of my decision to leave. He took the notification not unkindly, though there was quite understandably an undercurrent of irritation in his reply. I was to apply to the Superior-General of the order for a dispensation from the vows that I had somewhat hesitatingly taken some years before. During the wait for the decision from France I was to consider myself free from all obligations of attendance at lectures. I was to see of Rome what I had not already seen, and to enable me to do this P.P. was authorised to draw for me a small sum from the funds of the order. 'Enough money has been wasted on him already,' wrote the good old man. There was in that remark the bitter sting of truth.

The letter to the Superior-General was written, and I gave myself to an orgy of sightseeing. Spring was in the air: Mount Soracte's summit was no longer white; almost every day was a day of sunshine and of blue skies. What particular places I then saw I cannot now remember, and, anyhow, there have been sufficient guidebooks written about Rome.

A letter bearing the Paris postmark was handed to me at dinner one day towards the end of March, 1904. With affected indifference I stuck the letter in my soutane pocket. When, after dinner, I opened it, it contained two sheets of paper, which in all my wanderings I had carried about with me till they disappeared some years ago during a tidying-up by some member of my family. One in Latin, '*Dilecto nostro in Jesu Christo*,' declared me dispensed '*supra vota quae emisti in dicta congregatione*.' That is it released me from the vows I had made in the aforementioned congregation. The other in French was a little more explanatory: it said that the Superior-General, having read my letter and taken the advice of the Irish Provincial and of his Council, was sending me a dispensation from the vows I had made in the order. I was free, therefore, to leave it immediately. He was sending with me his affection, his regrets and his prayers that Our Lord would always have me in His holy keeping and give them the grace of meeting in Heaven.

The tears were close to falling as that night I drove through Rome to get the train for Paris and thereafter London. I was going home the cheapest way, on Cook's third-class vouchers. And certain incidents en route added to my conviction that the advice of the Franciscan had been the correct advice. When I reached Ireland, I was not so sure that it was. Ireland was the last place in which a 'spoilt priest' would be welcome. Its people had a supreme contempt for him that put his hand to the plough and then, as they said, let go of the handles.

6

That my immediate future was going to be unpleasant I was not left long in doubt.

On arriving at Dundalk I made at first for the village in which lived the relative who had whispered to me of her love for me. Chased from that village by a threat of being lynched, I sped as fast as I could for the thatched cabin in Carnally Rocks. I was there assured by my mother through her repressed tears that there would be a bite and a sup for me and the corner of a bed as long as there was a roof over her head. It was made plain to me, however, that I was 'on the shaughrawn', i.e. a jobless wanderer, and that it would have been easier for her, my brothers and sisters, if I had stayed away somewhere where nobody would ever hear or know anything about me.

Some miles away in a bleak little town under the dark Armagh mountains was a tailoring firm, the manager of which I persuaded to transform me in garb from the semblance of a cleric to that of a lay man. The manager had a long time to wait for the money. I sent it to him from South Africa.

The Franciscan colleges did not require any teachers. Nobody seemed to require a fellow like me. I tried to become an insurance agent, was given lists of 'prospects', sheets of policies. The 'prospects' would take one look at me and retort to my arguments, 'You're the young fellow who ran away from college, aren't you? No, thanks.'

Desperate, I crossed to Liverpool in the hope of finding work of some kind. In sultry June weather when the melting tar on the footpaths stuck to the soles of my boots I found out what it was to be hungry, made unwelcome acquaintance with the vermin and smells of a dosshouse, found the duck's breakfast, a drink of water and a walkabout, a most unsustaining repast, got a few shillings from an editor of a Catholic weekly for a column I wrote for him and, with my tail very much between my legs, made haste home to Carnally. I doubt if even the most glib-tongued Irishman – and I was far from being that – could have found work that summer in Liverpool for its streets were full of work-seeking men whose circumstances were as desperate as my own. Anyhow, I was learning the world the hard way.

I spent a couple of months in Carnally, taking my part in whatever farm work was to be done, learning that the reason for my having been sent to Rome was that the scandal I had given the previous summer had been so great that it was only the Pope who could give me absolution for it, that my loving relative had been for long a notorious priest hunter, that the disgrace I had brought on the Ballsmill Murphies was immeasurably greater than that brought on them by the 'Californian'. What the Californian Murphy had done I learned years afterwards during my return for a visit from South Africa. He had earned his sobriquet because, having fled from Ireland in the late forties of the nineteenth century, he had been in very early on the Californian gold rush of 1849, had amassed a fortune there – I have heard it claimed for him that he was the first man over the Rockies – and had returned with cartloads of gold to Ballsmill. The trouble with him was that he had tried to establish his own brothels amongst the Rocks. The people of the Rocks were not prepared for this advance in civilisation, and they had risen against the Californian and hunted him back to the States, in which he died in the late nineteenth century in the odours of wealth and sanctity.

Late in that autumn my mother proposed to me that I should go to the colonies. To which one? I was against going to America, Canada or Australia. Well, would I go to South Africa? I had no objection to that. As far as I knew there was nobody in South Africa who would think any the worse of me because I was a 'spoilt priest'. A friend of her girlhood days had two sons in good positions in Kimberley. She thought she could borrow the money for my passage thither and those boys would help me to get a job. I was to repay the money as soon as possible from my earnings.

With twenty pounds in my pocket I set out from Carnally for Kimberley. I had not the least notion how I was to get to Cape Town. I knew I could not swim to it. I made for Liverpool, guessing I would find in that city shipping offices in which I would be set on the right track. In them I learnt quite a lot about immigration laws, how, for instance, unless I had twenty pounds or a secure job to which to go, I would likely be returned to Europe as an undesirable. The clerk suggested I should in Liverpool purchase a Cook's voucher for my railway journey from the Cape to Kimberley. He advocated putting my pride in my pocket: I should make the sea part of the journey steerage. It would be rough going, but the clerk opined that at the other end two guineas extra, which a third cabin entailed, would be of great advantage to me.

So steerage it was; a bit rough certainly in the way of food, sleeping accommodation and the language and habits of my fellow steerage passengers. I learned from them that great kindness of soul may be accompanied by diction and morals of which the theologians whom for the past four years I had read so assiduously would not approve. About half of them were English and Welsh coalminers making their first venture to South Africa. Very few of them had the necessary twenty pounds laid down by the Cape immigration laws. Only a few of them had assured employment to which to go. So there was much speculative hope among them as to what would happen when Cape Town was reached. The other half of the steerage crowd were chaps who had spent years in South Africa, had thrown up their jobs in it and had been spending a summer in England. They felt assured about their being allowed to land, but were wondering deeply about what to head to in the search for work.

Among them I soon became known as 'Lucky Paddy'. In our

cramped quarters and with about as much deck space as would permit the lot of us to stand on it together if we shoved tightly against one another there could be no question of the ship's sports. We had instead an unending series of whist tournaments, a fresh one, I think, about every second day. I figured as the winner with, of course, a partner of most of them, not because I was a good whist player, but because I had extraordinary luck in the fall of the cards. Several times I had as many as twelve trumps. The others prophesied of me that I'd have a job within forty-eight hours of our getting to the Cape.

The trick of the shipping clerk at Liverpool came off. As the ship slid up to the docks at Cape Town, the immigration officials came on board, and we were all lined up alphabetically under a guard of stewards and ushered in before these dreaded beings one by one. I noticed several of those who went in before me come out with the tears rolling down their faces. It was a voyage back to England or Scotland for these poor devils. I had a breath-choking fear that I'd have a similar fate in front of me. When my turn came to be pushed into them, one of them barked at me:

'How much money have you got?'

'Two pounds fourteen shillings and three halfpence.'

'What?' he roared.

'And my ticket to Kimberley,' I hastily added.

'Show it,' he bellowed.

He examined it as if it were bound to be a fake. But, satisfied that it was a genuine voucher, he handed it back to me and said to the steward at the door:

'He's all right, steward. He can land.'

We landed on a particularly wet and windy Sunday morning for the month was October, just about the end of the Cape winter, which is the wet season for the Cape Town region of South Africa. And it rained for the better part of three successive days; rather it sleeted. We were travelling third on the Cape Railway system, and, as third-class was for Kaffirs, we were not very comfortable. It was perishingly cold the whole of that train journey. The other companies of the sea voyage left me at a junction called De Aar, as they were heading for the Rand, and I travelled on alone to Kimberley, not too hopefully most of the time.

If the prophesy about my getting a job within forty-eight hours of my landing in South Africa was not fulfilled to the hour, it was but a few hours over that figure before I was in employment. On my reaching the Diamond City I made my way to the fire station, where my young countryman commissioned by his mother to help me in my search for work explained to me that there was little scope in Kimberley for a fellow like myself, untrained to any trade, unversed in any commercial pursuit. My only chances were as a guard on De Beers' floors (and they were slight as, because of the prolonged drought prevailing about Kimberley that year, De Beers were actually discharging men as there was not enough water to run the diamond washing plant); in the police force, which just then had stopped recruiting for some time; or in the fire brigade. There might be a chance of a temporary job in it as at a fire a few nights previously a fireman had been injured. A report was awaited as to how long the injured man would be detained in hospital; if he were there for any length of time, a man would be appointed temporarily in his place, and I might get the job for a couple of months.

The report about the fireman came in next day. He would be out of action for three months, and the Mayor had authorised the appointment of a temporary fireman. I at once sought the brigade superintendent and pleaded for the temporary job. I had to plead as the superintendent considered I would be soft for the rough and dangerous work. I was fresh from school and I would very likely be unable to stand the rough life that men led. I told him that I was a lot tougher than I looked and that the prospect of three pounds a week – that was then the starting pay of a fireman – would brace me up for standing the life no matter how rough it was. I got the job, and, proving myself at a couple of pretty big fires to be as tough as anybody else, obtained a permanent appointment before the three months were up. I was, the superintendent commended, just what he liked one of his men to be: quick in action, utterly unafraid, yet cool-headed.

I remained in the brigade for eight years, rising to be second officer. The life at first was rough assuredly. The staff for a couple of years was mainly made up of old soldiers with a great capacity for lowering booze, but after that it primarily consisted of young Irish country lads, so much so in fact that the brigade became known as the 'Irish Brigade'. They were splendid chaps. Most of them are dead now, and my old eyes sometimes fill with tears as I think of the Nixons and the Evans, the Lennons, the Fogarties and Cremens with whom those years were passed. Horses were for six of these years used to draw all our machines. I learned to become a quite capable driver of all the machines, often doing a Ben-Hur act about Kimberley's tortuous streets in the early morning hours when the town was wrapped in a Stygian darkness and the only light I had was the faint flicker of oil lamps which reached only as far as the rumps of our beloved Diamond and Rooidam. When in about 1910 motor machines were brought in, I became a driver of them.

I got immersed too in a variety of sidelines that had nothing to do with fire brigade work, such as contributing to South African magazines and newspapers that went in for having a touch of literary flavour and acting as tutor in Latin, Greek, English and French to young fellows who had left school before taking their Matriculation. I thus earned a few pounds a week extra. The superintendent was fairly, indeed more than reasonably, generous, in allowing me time off for participating in what sport there was to be had in Kimberley. The sport *par excellence* was Rugby football. Kimberley was then a great stronghold of that game, for those were the days when the almost legendary 'Uncle Debbin', the great half-back of first and second Springbok teams to visit England, walked its streets. 'Klondyke' Raaf, Sid de Melker, his Jappie Marsburg comrades on the 1906 tour, as well as Billy

Martheze were then about the Diamond Fields, and young Sep. Ledger, Billy Delaney and Jack Braine, stalwarts of the 1912 tour, were fighting their way to the top. I started by practising Rugby as the officials of one of the local clubs, The Pirates, cajoled me into thinking that with my speed and strength there was a great future for me at the handling code. A crash tackle on me by Sep. Ledger, as I was making for the line in my second practice game, convinced me that a Rugby player would have to be extremely lucky if he lived long enough to make old bones. I turned to soccer, which was then, as were most other sports that weren't Rugby, looked on in Kimberley as no game for he-men, and was consequently having a rather desperate struggle to survive. Still, we soccer enthusiasts had our moments of glory. The team I joined never secured a listing far from the bottom of the league table of the Griqualand West Association table, but we became known as do-or-die cup-tie fighters, and we figured three years running in the local cup finals, winning twice. The 1907 final was a great thrill. It lasted throughout three Saturday afternoons with several periods of extra time. On the third Saturday we had a crowd of nearly ten thousand to watch us, and when we came out victors over a team of De Beers mechanics, among whom were a couple of ex-English professionals, the goalkeeper, the other fullback and myself were chaired off the field as the heroes of the game. The local paper on Monday mornings often had very flattering references to the rock-like defence of Murphy and his extremely clever defensive tactics.

I was for one of these years captain of a short-lived team of cross-country runners. I don't suppose I was ever Zatopek, but there was nobody around Kimberley just then who could keep with me at distances from five to twenty miles. I had the mad notion one of these years of entering for the South African trials for the Olympic marathon, but an injury to an ankle while leaping from a fire engine put an end to such an ambition.

I spasmodically played tennis of the pat or slash and scream variety. I was very good at the screaming.

About 1908 the Irishmen of the diamond fields started a Hurling Association, and for years the Irish national pastime was the one which claimed all my sporting ardour. I trained very assiduously for all the various forms of athletics and grew to be incredibly fit. I remember one weekend of these times during which I played two games of soccer and won a ten-mile cross-country race on the Saturday afternoon and played in a hurling match on the Sunday. Even on the Sunday night I was fit enough to fight a Tipperary chap with whom I had had some argument during the hurling game. Oddly enough the Hurling Association became the strongest sporting body around Kimberley. We would travel up to the Rand to play matches with the Gaels of the gold fields. The young colonials took to hurling as a duck takes to water, and several of them became nearly as good at it as were Irish-born fellows who had played in the Irish county teams before emigrating.

Another pastime we all shared at the fire station was that of falling in love. Though not born in golden climes with golden stars above, we were in love with love or more accurately with thinking ourselves in love. We called it square pushing, and the girl was known as the 'pusher'. On our rare periods off duty, we dolled ourselves in collars that came up to the ears and took our 'pushers' out, usually to the Kimberley public gardens, in which on certain evenings the band of the Kimberley Regiment under the direction of an Austrian called Herr Rybnikar, 'Ribs' to the less politely spoken of us, discoursed what I have no doubt was sweet music at open-air concerts. There in the glare of the arc lamps we strolled very important-looking around the bandstand, the 'pusher' clinging to our left arms while the right swung a cane almost as well as Charlie Chaplin was later on to swing his.

My first 'pusher' was a colonial lass named Amy. Tired of my quotations to her of long passages from Tennyson, she gave me the air after a few months. The next was a girl from Mayo who came out to Kimberley to help her sister in the running of a pub. The sister gave me the wipe there because I did not contribute enough to the pub sales. The third case, in which the young lady was a colonial girl, got to a really serious stage. It hung on for years, but her father, the descendant of English immigrants to South Africa almost a century before our time, would have none of me as a son-in-law. That was all the more remarkable as he was a Catholic and fiercely proud of the fact that all through the persecution of Catholics in England his ancestors had had the guts to stick by the ancient faith. It never occurred to him that the Murphies under such more violent persecutions than those endured by English Catholics must have had a considerable store of steadfastness to stand by theirs. He told me that he would rather see his girl married to a Kaffir than to me and so ballyragged the daughter that even on the morning of our wedding she withdrew from that decisive step. Perhaps he was right.

The life at the fire station was very restricted. Except when we had special permission to be absent from the station or on the Sunday following a turn of night-watch duty, we were on duty seven days of the week and for twenty-four hours a day. We had very little to do bar sit around waiting for the alarm to boom out its call to action. There was a little spit and polish to be done to engines and personal equipment. For the rest of the day we just sat at the front of the building in the winter mornings so as to catch the sunlight, at the back of it in winter afternoons so as to catch its heat. The reverse held good in summer. We had a rhyme:

'What's the fireman's occupation?
Chasing (or dodging) the sun around the station.'

We had an excellent recreation club in which there were a first-class billiard table and a very good library. We purchased quite a lot of boxing equipment. Not that any of us ever got to be much good at boxing, though we had a very fine instructor in the person of the superintendent, an Australian who had been taught the art by Jem Mace. A great South African sporting writer later told me that the skipper, had he stuck to fisticuffs, might have been the heavyweight champion of the world. This much I know: he had the kick of about ten mules in either hand. I saw it demonstrated on quarrel-seeking miners. A jab from him travelling no more than a few inches would put the sturdiest of them to sleep for half an hour. In his playful moods with us he would let his hands drop to his knees and offer a shilling for every time one of us could hit him anywhere on the head. I never saw him having to pay the shilling. Some of us were pretty hefty lads, well over six feet. As our blows seemed likely to connect there would be the faintest flick of his head, and the punch would travel harmlessly by him, missing him by inches. Of course, he was then in his forties and long past his best. But he had the ideal frame for a boxer: six feet two in height, fifteen stone weight, shoulders like a barn door and narrow hips. As an ex-boundary rider on Australian cattle ranges be could do anything with horses. May the earth rest lightly on Barney Doyle. He was ever my very good friend.

He taught me to use the typewriter, to keep the station accounts, and sometimes there was quite a lot of these to be kept, and quite a lot of correspondence with insurance companies. I thus had a number of reliefs from the ennui that beset us. I had others in that I made a number of friends in the households of my comrades on the football field. And yet others in the homes of the lads I was coaching. Very rarely were we free to accept invitations to social evenings. Such invites came from what might be looked on as the Pimlico rather than the Belgravia society of Kimberley. Very rarely did I accept of such proffered hospitality for I never had any social gifts, being unable to sing, make small talk, perform conjuring tricks or do anything to amuse. On the few occasions I went out I would have to sit through an evening like a bear with a sore head. The evenings when I had not a pupil I would mostly spend reading in my room. I read a tremendous lot in those years. There was then in Kimberley a very fine library, founded, I think, on a bequest made by Alfred

Beit, with a splendid selection of books. I admit that to be able to borrow books from it one had a to pay a small subscription, 5/- for three months if my memory is correct. So hardly were we pressed for time away from the station that I would often spend my meal hours in the library rambling round its ample shelves or sitting reading in its deep armchairs for it was a club room as well as a library for subscribers. There was one room in it for recreation: in it one could smoke, play games such as chess and draughts, and there was a veranda on which one could sit and read magazines and papers under an ample awning while fountains played on a grass lawn and on flower-beds. It was in every way a vast improvement on the forbidding public libraries to which one has to resort in London.

As to friendships, the closest I made was with the family of a German who was an official of moderately high ranking of the Kimberley Borough Council. He was married to a colonial lady descended from a Yorkshire family. I had got their youngest son over the hurdle of his Matriculation, a rather difficult job as though the lad could do almost anything with his hands he had very little capability in anything pertaining to book lore. In that home I was one of the family – 'Uncle' Pat to the younger girls thereof.

I should have been able to settle down contentedly to the life of a fireman, but as I look up a diary of the times I find that I was always wanting to get away from it. For a couple of years I partially succeeded in doing so. Under the impression that it would lead to a clerical post under the council I took the step of joining the Kimberley Borough Police. But I just became a member of about the oddest force that ever designated itself a constabulary. It consisted of six constables and a sergeant and had nothing whatever to do with the preservation of law and order. I think we were formally sworn in as constables, but we were really enlisted to enforce the sanitary bylaws of the council: to see that all food exposed for sale was in good condition and to collect the rates for such sanitary services as night soil removal (as the sanitation of Kimberley was then exclusively of the outside pattern), in short, to see to the cleanliness of the town generally. We had a long list of supplementary duties such as the capture by the aid of a posse of native constables of unlicensed dogs, inspection of rooms at night for overcrowding, disarming of natives and running around generally to appease citizens who complained of any failure on the part of the council to perform the removal of excrement, dust or slop-water. The disarming of natives was not so exciting as it reads. One of us just went about the streets accompanied by two native policemen, invariably two Zulus named Pompey and Thompson, in whose eyes the flame of battle lit up if they saw any 'dogs' – to them natives of any other race were 'dogs' – toting sticks around. I suppose there was a point in separating the 'dogs' from their sticks for when they had imbibed a few sups of Cape Dop or similar blood-stirring liquid they were inclined to test the sticks on one another's heads. True, it was generally the sticks that got broken in such exchanges, but even playful indulgence in such pastimes was inclined to lead to riots as the tribesmen of the attacked or an attacker were prone to take part in private fights. Pompey and Thompson carried their knobkerries (African clubs). When a 'dog' showed any reluctance to hand over his stick when ordered, the white constable made a signal for action by Pompey or Thompson. Both of the Zulus should have had their skill with a knobkerrie chronicled by a Haggard. A few passes by either of them round the head of the recalcitrant just made the latter's pugnacity vanish off the face of the earth. In a few hours' perambulation of the streets the 'cop sanitary' would have collected a great bundle of sticks, many of them very good ones. We were supposed to send these sticks to the Town Hall, where they would be made a bonfire of by the various uniformed flunkies that seem an adjunct of town halls. But we retained the best for ourselves and if we had no other distinction, when we went to the gardens of a Sunday night with our 'pushers', we would have the very finest of walking sticks as we escorted our Dulcineas round the bandstand.

Inspections for overcrowding were nearly always an unpleasant duty and occasionally apt to be dangerous. We were paid overtime for it and supposed to inspect a minimum number of rooms – I forget just what the number was. One may be sure it was rarely exceeded. We never entered the homes of white people, but there were plenty of premises occupied by coloured people: Negroes, half-castes, Asiatics of several breeds, such as Indians, Afghans, Chinese and Malays, the latter descendants of the slaves imported into South Africa in bygone ages by the Dutch. All through the town were dilapidated properties, condemned by the town engineer or the medical officer of health as unsafe or as unfit for human habitation. The owners were forbidden to let such buildings for accommodation, but as there was no rent control and they could charge what they liked for the lettings, a lot of such illicit letting went on. And the more people could be squeezed in, the greater the margin from which to meet fines. One would sometimes find Negroes just discharged from the mining compounds packed into these rooms like sardines in a tin. The reek of perspiration assailing one's nostrils as one went into such dens of a South African summer night is something I can still smell. The lodgers were usually drunk and would be annoyed at having their beauty sleep broken in upon. We would have our two Zulus strengthened for such inspections by their sergeant, a Cape Negro called Crottie, if his five feet of wiry black manhood could be regarded as a source of strength. He carried our measuring tape and a lantern, and when we thought there was overcrowding helped to measure up the rooms. Crottie, however, was a delightful companion as he was well versed in Bantu traditions. He had been educated in some mission school in the Cape Province. He both wrote and spoke English very well, though in an amusing way for he never used a short word while he had a chance of using a very long one. One of our fire tenders toppled over as it was sweeping round a corner one morning. Crottie who was riding on top of it, seemed not a whit the worse for his having been thrown off about twenty yards and landing on his head. Later on in the morning I expressed to Crottie my hope that he was none the worse for this misadventure. 'In no wise,' he assured. 'By the omnipotent and omnipresent Almighty's oversight of the most insignificant of His creatures I was projected earthwards on my occiput.' Crottie was a fine Christian, but I always had my doubts whether his Christianity or his sesquipedalian verbiage would have been of much help to us on overcrowding inspections were the disturbed Negroes to turn awkward. When danger was expected myself and a giant from Fermanagh were assigned to the work. I had acquired a natty revolver and always displayed it on such occasions.

Sometimes we would arouse a coloured prostitute and the man who was pleasuring with her. Then the language was 'frequent and painful and free'. Often the lady would leap from her bed in her birthday attire and tell us in the choicest of abusive language just where we should go to.

We had the power of arrest, but very rarely exercised it. Whenever we did so it was because a man summoned to the magistrate's court for offences against the sanitary regulations or for non-payment of sanitary rates had omitted to appear and so became guilty of contempt of court. Then orders went out for his arrest. Usually the big Fermanagh man and myself were sent to make the arrest. Once we had to arrest one of De Beers' mining officials. We went to the mine, had the man brought out to us at the gate and explained to him just why the magistrate would like to have a few words with him. The man was one of a crowd then in Kimberley known as 'Rhodes's pensioners', that is fellows who had done Rhodes some service in return for which C.J.R. enjoined that they were ever to be kept in a good job in the mighty diamond concern. The pensioner showed not the least annoyance about it all, just requested that we would walk through the town ten or twenty yards behind him. We agreed to that. What we had not reckoned on was that this fellow had once broken records at track walking. He nearly pulled the legs off both of us. The magistrate fined him one pound for his contempt. He most cheerfully paid the fine and then took the pair of us to one of Kimberley's flash hotels and stood us most noble whiskies and sodas.

We got commission on our collections. If one were energetic, one could easily earn about a quid a week from these collections. We remained attached to the fire brigade as auxiliary firemen, getting paid 12/6 a week for that and having a free room at the fire station. Often we got two turns of overcrowding inspection per week; another 10/-. Taking it altogether we were earning very good wages. Against that was to be set the fact that we were the most unpopular men in Kimberley, the legion of the despised, if there ever was one. And we might also be called on for all other kinds of unpleasant duties. Thus on a few occasions the coloured foremen of the w.c. removal gangs went on strike and the municipal police were called on to act as strike breakers. On each one of these occasions some opponent on the football field had the kindly foresight to bust up my ankle or knee, and as such I managed to escape having to endure the various smells by which the night air was made malodorous. The worst that fell to me in these extraneous duties was to act as barman when the Mayor made festivities with the higher ranks of the council staff. Another cop and myself got our own back by putting a strong purgative in the drink of my official who had made himself obnoxious to us.

Another occasion I remember very clearly was standing in the blazing sun in uniform while the council entertained the Kimberley children in the public gardens (now, I understand, named Hoffe Park) at the celebration of what, I think, was the first Empire Day. And, what was still worse, I had to listen to the speeches the bigwigs made at the end of the day.

In the years 1907 to 1908 Kimberley went through a very lean period. The mines practically closed down because of a slump in America, which had provided the best market for diamonds. Thousands of miners and their ancillaries were discharged and those who remained were put on short time. Kimberley bade fair to see realised a prophecy attributed to Rhodes that grass would grow in its streets. Trade was very badly hit except that of auctioneers. Houses were empty in every street; rates fell almost to a trickle, and it became a matter of interest to us 'sanitary cops' what the borough council, faced with the loss of half its revenue through closed-up residences and bankrupt business premises, was going to do in the way of retrenchment. It did quite a lot. It cut all salaries by ten per cent. Its municipal police got a second, a third and even a fourth swing of the axe. The collections of sanitary rates were taken from us on the grounds that they could be effected more cheaply by two salaried and fidelity-bonded collectors for the whole town. Various duties for which we had been paid overtime were in future to be done for the good of the town, and our basic salary of three pounds per week got the general ten per cent cut. Our earnings dropped by fifty per cent. Though small in numbers, we had become a noble band of brothers. Practically the lot of us resigned. Some headed out for the Rand; others made for Australia. The Fermanagh giant headed for New Zealand, where, I learned years afterwards, he became an important figure in the police force. I, liking to venture alone, was on the point of going up to Rhodesia, where, because of my football ability, small though it was, I was assured of a job. Just then the superintendent of the fire brigade, making some changes in his firefighters, persuaded me to return to the fire station as a full-time fireman with an officer's status. I accepted. Thus I returned once more to dodge or chase the sun around the station.

7

Looking back on things, I often wish I had been content to stay where I was, but scanning faded notes of my life about then, I seem to have, after the first month or so, been devising plans by which I could get away from what was then Stockdale Street. The first plan that flickered through my mind was to take a course at the Cape University, get a degree and become a schoolteacher. I was muchly urged to do so by the parents of the young people whom I was tutoring. There was then – still is, I am told – a secondary school in Kimberley called the Christian Brothers' College. All the staff of it were Irish, and, through playing football against and with some of its boys and staff, I had come to have an acquaintance with its principal. I sought his advice about the schoolmastering idea. 'Break stones first,' said he.

I played with the idea of becoming a diamond prospector. In my reading of South African history and native legends I had come across the legend that there was an immense deposit of diamonds somewhere about the Great Falls of the Orange River. I would go away into the desert, find these diamonds, come back to Kimberley and hold De Beers to ransom. Closer inquiries about the nature of the country in which the diamonds were to be found convinced me that, greenhorn as I was to the ways of the desert, I would be more likely to leave my bones bleaching in the desert after the vultures had gorged themselves on my flesh than to emerge from it with sackfuls of diamonds. The diamonds, to be picked up in bucketfuls, have since been found along the Orange, but by the time the aeroplane had made possible the transport of the gems to civilisation I was a warder in an English

61

prison, dreaming of equally hare-brained ways of reaching out for fortune.

I very seriously considered going into partnership with some chaps who owned or had options over some goldbearing properties in Bechuanaland. At first that seemed very attractive to me, but friends pointed out that if the gold was there in payable quantities, the land would likely have been snapped up by Rhodes or some other of the gold magnates instead of being allowed to fall into the possession of couple of ex-officers of somewhat dubious reputation. The gold was there, true enough, but the ore was refractory and could not be refined except at a cost which made its working prohibitive. The idea was that I, being a clever sort of youth, should after learning a bit about the practical working of a mine – there was one of sorts on the property – go on to the School of Mines in Johannesburg, become versed in metallurgy and then find a process by which the ore could be handled at payable cost. A sort of new cyanide process, by which the Rand gold production was saved in the early days. My would-be partners were silent as to who would stand expenses while I was thus fitting myself to turn them and me into other Beits and Robinsons, and the discovery that one of them regarded it as a clever trick to toss for drinks with a double-headed or double-tailed penny made me reflect that I was very likely to come out on the losing end of the deal. I gave a very decided and definite 'No' to the offer, and soon the syndicate folded up. Of course, none foresaw the likelihood of the British Empire going off the gold standard. The price of raw gold was then fixed: since it has become free the price is what one can get for it; about three times as much as back in 1909.

The fatal break with what might have been a quiet, if a bit monotonous, life, with peaceful and comfortable retirement came through the wholly mistaken notion that arose within me that I had it in me to become a journalist. I was never likely to be half as good a journalist as I was a fireman. I continued with my coaching and with my contributions to South African magazines and papers, some of which paid and some did not. The paper to which I made most of my contributions was one of those that did not. It was a weekly appearing on Saturday nights, owned by a Northumbrian who had a stationery and job printing business in Kimberley. It was edited by a man whose acquaintance with journalism was almost as theoretical as my own, but he was making such a success of the job that he began to dream of its blossoming out into a daily evening paper. He persuaded the proprietor to cherish the same vasty dream. Both, in view of the amount I had written for the weekly, promised me, on condition that I learnt shorthand, a job on the evening paper as sub-editor and special reporter. At the same time, having served with the council for over seven years without any official holidays (though as a matter of fact I had had in that time two holidays given me without the council's knowledge by the superintendent), I applied in 1912 for a six months' leave and got it on full pay. I set out from Kimberley with letters of introduction to the 'nobs' of some of the London dailies, was very kindly received by them, especially by a man named Stewart, the foreman printer of what was then *The Daily News* and *Morning Leader*. I saw everything with the eyes of the castle builder and formed for myself visions of our new evening paper with its Linotypes changing sheets of my 'copy' into lead-lettered columns and rotary machines churning out thousands of copies of our paper every hour. I went over to Ireland in great humour with myself. When I got back to South Africa, I would be a somebody.

The Carnally Rocks had been so changed that as I viewed them from a hillside over the old road that led into them I at first thought I had come to the wrong district. Seven years had made my mother grey and stiff, but she thanked God in that He had spared her to see my return. Now, she said, I could hold up my head and look my detractors in the face. I wore what for me were good clothes, had quite a few pounds of my own in my pocket or in the bank. I had a motorbike bicycle, bought in London, to enable me to see Ireland in style, and so the people

were now as anxious to look up to me as they had previously
been to scorn me.

Motorbike and all, I did not see much of Ireland that holiday.
The year 1912 remains in the minds of the folk of South Armagh
as the wettest and coldest summer in living memory. It rained
two days out of three. I spent most of my time looking out from
the half-door at the mists that drifted round the tops of the
mountains, and even when there came a dry day the machine
proved very unreliable, making of long-distance journeys by it
things of high adventure.

On one trip on it I got as far as Belfast, outside which my
younger brother was the foreman on a large farm. On a dreary
day we went into that very dreary city. Rain was pouring down
onto its sloppy streets, along which, on the afternoon of July
12th, marched a hundred thousand Orangemen yelling about their
Covenant. They were headed by Carson and 'Galloper' Smith on
horseback, rather like two sacks of wet meal dumped onto the
backs of their sorrowful-looking steeds. They were the most
unmilitary figures that ever led a march of contingent rebels. I
have often since wondered what bloodshed Ireland might have
been spared had the government had the courage to clap that
pair into prison. For their antics were the beginning of great evils
to that unhappy land.

When in September I got back to Kimberley, my dreams of
our new paper proving anything like the thing I had been imagining
it would be got immediately shattered. Worse still, life at the fire
station was far from being the comfortable, friendly life it had
been. No man had done more to keep the Irish together as a
sporting and social body than had the superintendent. They had
quarrelled with him because he would not allow them to use the
brigade's recreation room as a place for gambling. I'm probably
the only Irishman ever born with an antipathy to cards. As one
of them once said to me my dislike of them is possibly due to
my not having brains enough to play them. Anyhow, there it
was. It was no longer an exclusively Irish fire brigade that leaped

for the machines when an alarm sounded and went tearing hell for leather round the Kimberley streets. Apart from the superintendent no longer being so keen to engage young Irish chaps for it, the council had let it be known it was time for young colonials to be given a chance in it, and on the resignation of some of the Hibernians a number of Kimberley-born youths had been taken on the strength. They had not the elan of submissiveness to an iron discipline possessed by the Irish. They were ever asking for time off to attend to family affairs such as running messages or shopping for their mothers. Quite often they'd not bother to ask for time off for such purposes, and were rather inclined to do their courting in the firm's time. The result of this was that often our crews were short on our turning up to a fire and extra work was thrown on to us. The Irish who had remained on in the brigade demanded that the colonials must toe the line, and so there was an almost constant bickering between the two sections of the staff or between one of them and the superintendent.

Preparations for the launching of the evening daily went forward very slowly. The Northumbrian was short of capital: there would be no Linotypes or rotary printing presses. He just could not manage them. All he would be able to furnish in the way of new plant would be a single typesetting machine worked somewhat after the fashion of a Linotype but bearing as much resemblance to it as a lame cat bears to a frisky lion. He'd have a new printing press, electrically operated, and, it is true, a vast improvement on the old one with which he had been turning out the weekly, but still a flat-bedded creaking sort of thing. As for reporters I'd be the only one. I would *ex officio* be sub-editor, but I'd be reporter and proofreader and was to do a bit of advertisement canvassing as well. The service from the news agencies – I think Reuters Ltd was the only one – would be on the very lowest scale. Scissors and paste or the ingenuity of myself and the editor would have to fill in the gaping columns. And he had only been able to get thus far by mortgaging his home. I had read somewhere that the proprietor of a new paper had to be prepared to face the loss of a million in the first year; with the Northumbrian it seemed as if the loss of five quid in that time would bring on disaster. Even to me the chances of success for our evening paper under these circumstances looked hopeless, and what made them worse was that it was not really going to be an evening daily as it would appear only on three evenings a week. The Northumbrian could not stand up to the wages bill entailed by a daily edition. I had some friends among the editors of other South African papers. They had been dangling prospects of journalistic employment at the Greek Calends, it seemed to me. They and other friends advised me to have nothing to do with the tri-weekly. It was neither fish nor fowl nor red herring, they said.

But I disregarded all advice about continuing to wear out the seat of the council's heavy black trousers by remaining at the fire station till a better chance turned up. The wages offered by the Northumbrian were nominally a bit higher than those I had been getting in the fire brigade. I was in one of my love of love moods just then, the most serious one, and I understood from the girl that her people would withdraw their objections to me if I got myself a real job. The proposed sub-editorship seemed to me a way to come up to their demands for respectability, and there was something romantic about the acceptance of it. I had developed a close liking for and friendship with the editor. I had also developed a dislike for the two reporters for the morning daily of the town. I felt it was up to me to get my own back on them for some slights I imagined they had put upon me, when, trying my prentice hand at reporting, I had once or twice taken a seat with them at the reporting table. I felt I owed to things in general to work off a spite for having plashed a way to even a mediocre knowledge of shorthand. We would likely fall, I recognised, but it would be glorious to have tried in face of all the chances of success being against us.

So about Easter, 1913, I told the proprietor I would be his to command from July 1st, the date on which the first number of the tri-weekly was to appear. There would be a lot of preliminary work to do in the way of preparation for that event in the journalistic world. I offered to assist in this preparation at my own expense or rather at the expense of the Kimberley Borough Council as I would get my annual three weeks' holiday to start from the 7th of June and that three weeks I would devote to assisting the Northumbrian and the editor to getting things moving. My application for the leave was granted. At midnight on the eve of the day on which it was to start we had an alarm of fire. I drove our first tender to that fire, a small one as it happened, and at 9 a.m. on the next morning planked myself on the chair in the office that was to serve 'Pat' Murphy and Digby Filer as the editorial sanctum in which they would make a new venture in South African journalism.

It was as different as possible from the editorial sanctum – or should it be sancta? – into which I had got a glimpse when I was passing through London. Instead of being in the well-ventilated, wainscotted room of my dreams we were in a cubby-hole that had been used as a lumber room for job printing. There was one window that started about two feet from the ground and faced west. There was no fireplace in it. We froze in winter and were parboiled in summer. A couple of rude cupboards had been set up in a corner. There was not a single reference book of any kind in the room. I fetched a couple of my own dictionaries and an oil stove of my own into it. For the three weeks I read proofs, reported meetings for the old weekly, canvassed for advertisements for the tri-weekly, heard with what patience I could master the blasphemies of the hand-setting compositors and listened to the stories of his world wanderings told by the German who set up the new machinery. A lot of the stories were about Ireland and Australia, in both of which countries he had set up for little provincial papers his imitation of the Linotype. I had uneasy feelings that I had not acted very wisely in resigning from the fire brigade and to make the best of a bad job I threw myself with zest into all these preparatory moves.

8

The first Saturday night of July, 1913, was marked by the launch of the new tri-weekly to the public of the diamond fields. We had been looking forward with much trepidation, yet with some spasms of hope, to that first issue. Weeks of canvassing by the Northumbrian, Filer and myself had ensured for it a good advertising revenue for its first three months. The attitude of the public, though not warm enough for the investment of capital in the enterprise, had been encouraging. The morning daily was looked upon – rightly or wrongly, I do not know – as tied up with De Beers, and there was beginning to spread over Kimberley some faint breath of opposition to monopolistic concerns. It was a breath, no more, but it was perceptible and working ever so slightly in our favour. Socialism was being preached in the town, and though the tri-weekly was a capitalist production, it was felt that it was not as much tainted with capitalism as was a paper that was linked with a huge mining concern.

The Northumbrian was himself a bit of a Radical, not a very definite bit, and he had been irritated by having it conveyed to him that some of the diamond magnates did not regard very favourably his new venture into newspaper production. Dammit! He was a Geordie lad, and he'd start what he pleased. It was his money, wasn't it? Filer was seriously a Radical, if not a socialist, in his views. He loved to tell how as a youth of twenty he had played some part in the London Dock Strike of 1889, had been by the side of John Burns at the famous Trafalgar Square meeting, how he had the hand of Ben Tillett placed in approbation on his shoulder. I wasn't anything in particular just then; just instinctively opposed to big bugs, fond of a row of any kind and meaning to be in any that were knocking about.

The birth pangs of the paper were fierce with the result that it did not appear until some hours after the time arranged. The newly installed machinery was slow in working itself in. Outside in the street an enormous crowd was clamouring for the paper's appearance. When the rag at last got off the press, copies were snapped up as fast as they could be passed out. We all turned to and lent a hand in the sale of the damp sheets. Copies for subscribers – there were not many unfortunately – had to be smuggled out by a back way. At 11 p.m. Filer and I went off, leaving the Northumbrian, his wife and a couple of the shop-girls totting up receipts of threepenny bits. We might be pardoned for cozening ourselves into hope of success.

Fortune had played into our hands to some extent. The Rand miners had gone on strike that week, had got out of hand on the Friday, on the afternoon and night of which there had been arson and looting in Johannesburg. On the Saturday there had been shooting. Mind you, we knew very little of the details of what was happening in the City of Gold. A censorship had been imposed there – I guess Jan Smuts [South African statesman, general and prime minister from 1919 to 1924] was behind that – and little or nothing came through in the way of press news. But a couple of Kimberleyites who had been spending their holidays on the Rand had hared back to Kimberley at the first signs of trouble on the Friday. On the Saturday they sped round to us to give us their tales. Other Kimberley folk had had letters from relatives in the strike area on the Saturday morning, and they made themselves important by coming round to our cubby-hole and letting us make extracts from these letters. Some Kimberley traders had had during the day snatches of telephone conversation with their opposites on the Rand, and they gave us the benefit of their versions of the disturbances. Filer and I, both gifted with lively imaginations and able from our knowledge of Jo'burg to splash in plenty of local colour, made a passably good job of writing up all this stuff and setting it down, of course, as 'From our own correspondent'. Yet when some days later the full facts of the rioting came out, we had not very far overstepped reality in our pictures of blazing hotels and newspaper offices, looted stores and British soldiers kneeling in the street to shoot down the strikers. The populace rejoiced that Kimberley had at last a live paper!

The esteem we won through the strike affair and our handling of it, for, of course we cried out against tyranny and senseless bloodshed, carried the tri-weekly along in pretty good style for a few weeks. Looking back on our first month, Filer and I felt that if we had not soared to the summit of our first night's hope, we had not done too badly and that, if we had an adequate news service and sound, instead of chancy, business management behind us, we would ride joyously to success. We had a market, but could not deliver the goods.

The news service was maddeningly poor, especially on items of overseas news, on which we got but very condensed summaries of what took up columns in our wealthy morning rival. The Northumbrian averred that he could not afford another 'tickey' (threepenny piece) on news services. All we got could often be put into a couple of columns of our twelve pages had we not been very generous in our headings, even with the utmost of our informative additions for the enlightenment of our readers. They very soon made known to us that they sought facts not information and that they were weary of rereading in our numbers things they had already read in other papers. In the circumstances we had to fill in a lot with cuttings from our 'exchanges'. The half column we always reserved for 'Stop Press' news became a standing joke against us. I think in all the nine months we were on the rag we only once had even a line of what we called 'fudge'.

Our advertisement and sales departments were after the first burst run on very haphazard lines. The Geordie and his bookkeeper did, it is true, some 'going after ads', but this effort on their part tended to narrow down to pleading with an advertiser for a repeat of an ad that had already appeared in the morning paper. The sales side was worked just as chancily. True, Geordie had a dozen or so dirty, ragged half-breeds who scampered round the streets making a great noise and picking up stray 'tickeys' for our as yet damp sheets, but we often found his wife bewailing that one or more of the 'boys' had levanted with the 'tickeys'.

However in September we had a rather glorious time while it lasted. Kimberley was to be amalgamated with the adjoining township of Beaconsfield, and the result was to be the City of Kimberley and Beaconsfield. I wonder if the Beaconsfield has since been dropped. The parish pump politicians worked up a respectable show of excitement over this amalgamation. Elections were to be held for the twelve seats on the new city council, and nearly forty candidates representing this, that and the other thing, but mostly representing themselves, presented themselves for the approval of the citizens. The daily and ourselves, so far bitter rivals, came strangely enough to an agreement about how to treat these aspirants for civic honours. Each would charge the same rate for notices about the election. Neither would accept a notice unless it was guaranteed that it would be inserted in the other. It was made known that candidates who did not advertise freely would stand small chance of having their meetings reported. Revenue simply poured in. It poured in also to the jobbing side of Geordie's business. All the candidates flooded the electorate with handbills. Whatever effect this outpouring of handbills had on the electorate, it made life busy for the street cleaners.

The bulk of reporting the meetings fell on me, and I enjoyed it. I guessed that descriptive touches on the mannerisms and eccentricities of the speakers would make much spicier reading than would long accounts of what the Simple Simons proposed doing to make Kimberley a better place in which to live and die. All of them became anxious to stand in my good graces so that they might escape my irreverent digs.

Filer got the idea that it would be a good thing to act out a special eve-of-the-poll edition, in which each of the candidates would make a final statement of his views and aims. Each of them, if he paid the cost of the block, would have his photograph inserted. I interviewed all the candidates for this final statement. It was great fun. One dear old chap assured the public, through me, that he had been for forty years burying the people of Kimberley and that he had not had a single complaint about his work. If elected, he would continue to give the Kimberleyites satisfactory burial.

The climax of the interviews was to be with the man, now a world figure in finance, who, having been Mayor of the defunct Kimberley Borough Council and the prime mover in the amalgamation, was certain of election and almost certain to be the first Lord Mayor. This was to be a very serious interview, but it turned out to be the most ridiculous of the lot. The proof was to be submitted to the great man for his approval. Filer came along with me to the interviewing. Filer put him a number of questions, and I in my still rather slow shorthand took down the answers of the oracle. He gave the proof an enthusiastic OK.

The element of the ridiculous came through the foreman printer's flurry in the make-up of the edition. In among the columns of the interview he allowed to creep lines and even 'sticks' of an advertisement for a patent medicine. The new Lord Mayor was made to seem to say that the best thing he could do for the Kimberley folk was to keep their bowels moving freely.

The elections were almost our last little gleam of triumph. After them the *Star* sloped steadily towards the west. At the end of three months several of the big advertisers refused to renew their contracts. Sales fell off rapidly. One could feel that the 'caps' for the tri-weekly's epitaph were due to be set any day. It became a question of when the thing would fold up completely. We got our pay cheques round about midday on the Saturday. Once I got my fingers on mine I dashed round to the bank and cashed it.

At the end of the year the *Star* took a more decided plunge towards failure when the six-monthly advertising contracts ran out and the advertisers declined to renew them. The Northumbrian's wife now took charge of the business. She was an excellent businesswoman, and perhaps her energy did ultimately succeed in pulling things round. For all I know, the paper may still be running. Filer's and my connection with it came to a sudden end at the end of January, 1914. Poor Filer was killed in German West Africa the April of 1915.

The big excitements of January were the visit of an M.C.C. team to Kimberley and renewed labour troubles on the Rand. The cricket team came, saw and conquered. That was only to be expected. Kimberley, though in the early days it gave a Tancred and a Shalder to South African cricket and, in later days, a Balaskas, has never been a stronghold of the game. [English captain Johnny] Douglas was very determined to win. Incidents occurring on that tour were provocative of nearly as much ill-feeling as that resulting from the tour of Jardine's team in Australia eighteen years later. The visit of the team to Kimberley brought me the pleasure of lunch with Lionel Tennyson and Jack Hobbs, in their very different ways as fine examples of the sporting spirit as could be met with. Other members of the team were very definitely the reverse.

The labour trouble on the Rand this time had something to do, oddly enough, with Rugby football. It spread very rapidly from mine to mine for the miners, sore over their defeat the previous July, were eager for any excuse for an all-out struggle with the mine owners. Their leaders fanned resentments by the addition of other pretexts and the deprivation of amenities for playing and watching Rugby until the strike culminated in the proclamation of a general stoppage of labour and a call for the workers of other centres to show solidarity and come out in support of their fellows on the Rand. The government – slim Jannie Smuts got the credit for being the government – replied by the proclamation of martial law all over the gold-fields, and threatened its extension to any other centres of the Union in which trouble broke out. The Defence Forces were called out everywhere. The strikers tried desperately to paralyse transport by appealing to the railwaymen to come out, and the government countered this by putting on all trains a couple of armed guards, and these guards, drawn from local defence units, conveyed very strongly that they would not hesitate to demonstrate the uses to which rifles and ammunition could be put. A faint attempt was made to embroil De Beers' employees in the turmoil, but to the intense disappointment of Filer and myself the attempt did not develop the strength of a dung beetle pushing a lump of muck in front of it. A few would-be Kimberley strikers lost their jobs, and that was the end of that. The men of De Beers knew they were under a benevolent labour tyranny, and benevolence counted more with them than did the brand of crude Marxism preached from the Rand.

Our rival went strongly against the strike; we went just as strongly in favour of it. I hadn't the faintest interest in the right or wrong of the dispute, but deemed that backing the strikers would yield much more fun than would backing the mine bosses. Having been recognised as having a gift of sarcasm, I was commissioned to think out spiteful things to say of the latter and of the Union government. When the government, as I now think, quite rightly threw sixty thousand Dutch commandos round Johannesburg and, placing artillery round the city's Trade Hall, gave the pinchbeck revolutionary leaders twenty-four hours in which to surrender or be blown to pieces, we shrieked of a new model Zabernism and ranted about tyranny. All this sent the tri-weekly sales up with a rush. That was what we most cared about.

The Northumbrian protested that we were going too far, but we went on going. There is no doubt that if martial law had been proclaimed in Kimberley, we would very likely have been jailed. We ridiculed the local leaders of the Defence Force, likening them to strutting Prussian lieutenants and wanting to know where they had left their duelling marks.

When the strikers' leaders, preferring surrender to being blown to blazes, were deported without trial, we howled about habeas corpus and Magna Carta. When the tumult was dying down, we staged a two-man strike. One Saturday evening the Northumbrian, telling us that the paper was not paying its way, a thing we knew only too well, asked us to accept cuts in our wages. On the Monday we sent him a joint letter to inform him that if by the following Saturday, he did not intimate to us that the old wages would still be paid we would walk out. He did not, and the following Saturday we saw the rag to press, tore up all reserve copy, mostly more scissors and paste stuff, walked out the back way, had a drink and told ourselves what heroes we were.

We wandered about Kimberley on the Monday, the recipients of much sympathy from the more liberally minded sections of the populace, who held that the reduction of pay had been prompted by the diamond bosses as a punishment for the attitude we had taken up during the strike. That, I feel sure, was quite unfounded. I did not think we were important enough to have anybody bother about us. Still, it was rather pleasant to be looked on as a sturdy Briton suffering in the cause of the downtrodden, and for me it was not so utterly miserable to be without a job as I had feared it would be. I had no ties in Kimberley; of my last year in it I had some memories from which I was anxious to separate myself. Filer was, however, in a more desperate position. He had a wife and four young children dependent on him. My position in the fire brigade had not as yet been filled, and I suppose I could have gone back to it with my tail between my legs or secured some lowly position in De Beers, no more than that of a guard on the mine floors.

Filer proposed various schemes by which, he thought, we might continue to work together in Kimberley. We'd constitute ourselves a journalistic syndicate, sending contributions to all the South African dailies and weeklies. I couldn't see very much hope of success at that game. He next opined that the time had come for a South African labour daily and felt sure that the then leader of the South African Labour Party would back us up morally and financially. I had already met this leader and thought him very much a leader from the rear. I did not think he would have the strength of mind to back up anything. Money he certainly hadn't got, and we'd need a lot of money to start a daily.

One day I went back to the office to collect from it my oil stove and my dictionaries. The Northumbrian came on me while I was wrapping up the books and invited me to return to him as editor, reporter, general factotum on the paper. He would increase my wages by one pound a week. He felt sure that, as I had been doing most of the work on it during the past months, I'd be able to carry it out entirely by myself. The money saved by not having Filer's wages to pay would put the paper on a paying basis. I declined, not in doubt that I could do all he stated, but I'd be going behind Filer's back in a particularly mean way.

A few minutes later I was cycling past the Post Office. A desire to see what other parts of the world were like, to have a wider experience of life seized me. I jumped off the bike, went in and wired to the Cape Town office of Thos. Cook:

'Book me berth on first boat leaving Cape Town anywhere but England.'

Within an hour I had the reply:

'Berth booked *Berrima* leaving for Sydney, February 2nd.'

These were the days when in the deservedly classical words of Ernest Bevin one could go wherever the hell one liked. I caught the *Berrima*, and travelled on her to Sydney in company with four hundred of the Rand strikers and three hundred male and female emigrants from all over Great Britain. The emigrants were mostly females, and I learned quite a lot about life on that voyage. And within the next two years I was to learn quite a bit about death.

9

The most vivid impressions I retain of Sydney during the month I spent in it, while I was trying to find for myself a niche in a new world, were those of the cheapness and high quality of food, and the extraordinary kindness of the people whom I approached for a job.

For my last two years in Kimberley I had frequented cafes for meals, often getting indifferent and costly ones, but preferring those with a book to read while eating to the affected conversation with which I had been afflicted in some of its boarding-houses. In Sydney there were cafes in which one might have a good, clean meal for sixpence. I had got myself a bedroom in a house out Darlinghurst way and had all my meals out. Breakfast never cost me more than sixpence. After a swim in one of the inlets of the famous harbour I'd have porridge and milk, bacon and eggs, while it was nobody's business but my own how much I'd have in the way of bread and butter, jam and tea. Down in the city while a perfectly good lunch might be had for the same small sum, I'd sometimes treat myself to one costing ninepence. For either sum one could have four courses with the usual extras eaten off spotlessly clean table linen, while around would be a confusing array of cutlery and condiments. All that, I expect, is another part of a lost world.

Though I had not come to Australia with intentions limited to journalism as a means of livelihood, I thought I had better see what possibilities there might lie ahead of me in that line. I had provided myself with a very fine testimonial written by myself and signed by Filer, showing that I had had a wide and long experience in all phases of journalism. I rather timorously set about offering my services to the editors of the Sydney papers. I was met everywhere with a civility that made inability to give a job seem more of a sorrow to the editor than to the applicant. In Sydney a commissionaire's business seemed to be rather to help an applicant to see the person he asked to see than to hunt him off. The editor of the *Sydney Bulletin* chatted with me for over an hour and sent out for coffee. The editor of a daily bade me drop in any time for a talk. He professed himself intensely sorry that just then he had no vacancies, but he might hear of one on some upcountry paper, and he might be able to help me to pull off a job. A press association went so far as to circulate my testimonial to its clientele. So, if a job was not materialising, I had hopes of one dangling in front of me and saw no immediate necessity to buy myself a pick and shovel so that I could qualify an an applicant for membership of one of the navvy gangs for which recruits were daily being sought in the small advertisements of the press.

In the intervals of calling on editors and writing articles on aspects of the Australian scene for South African papers, which had assured me of favourable consideration of anything I would send them in that line and would one day bring grist to my mill, I wandered around the city and its environs always finding something new and interesting. One great novelty for me was to see rain pelt down on the streets steadily for a whole fortnight. That, after the burning droughts of South Africa interspersed with tropical deluges, was interesting, if a trifle uncomfortable. Another contrast with the semi-desert regions around Kimberley was wandering about the beaches at Coogee, Bondi and Botany Bay.

Hopes have a habit of fading away like snow in sunshine. When the pick and shovel career or rabbit snaring (with or without experience) began to assume closer personal interest than simply as a phenomena of labour conditions. I noticed that applications were being invited for the editorship of a Catholic weekly in Brisbane. A knowledge of Catholic theology and philosophy would be a distinct advantage. Just the chance for a 'spoilt priest', thought

I, and decided I'd have a run up to the Queensland capital and try to land the job. I went up by coastal steamer, on which were travelling numbers of those aristocrats of labour, the sheep-shearers, to the great sheep stations of Western Queensland.

Little did I think, as the boat cut its way through the beds of hyacinth and the masses of jellyfish floating down the Brisbane River that I should soon be outward bound down it on a much larger boat with my destination Berlin.

I spent my first week in Brisbane working up what points I could to secure the editorship of that weekly. I was 'full feebly friended' for I knew not one person in the whole of Australia. I was quite kindly received by its directors and thought the job was mine until in stepped another 'spoilt priest', more recently spoilt than I, just fresh out from Ireland and having behind him a thunderously imposing uncle in the person of parish priest on the outskirts of the city. He got the editorship.

There was another, much smaller, Catholic weekly in Brisbane. It was family owned and family run. The father, white of beard and very patriarchal in appearance, was the editor; the son, as well as looking after sales and advertisements, often took his stand at the 'box', while the daughter kept the accounts. They had been employing an outside reporter, a non-Catholic, to supply reports of Catholic functions and meetings. This work they transferred to me. Pay 10/6 a report. There were special articles to be written from time to time, and I got the half-guinea for each one I wrote. They also recommended me to a priest who was trying to raise funds for the repair of his own church by writing a history of the Catholic Church in Brisbane. He gave me the job of devilling out the thing in rough form. It was not hard or uninteresting work. It was mainly a matter of getting in touch with a parish priest and persuading him to tell the story of the early struggles of his mission and making extracts from the parish records if there happened to be any. The priests were mostly Irish, and it was not a hard matter to enlist their co-operation. None talked more freely or went to greater length to help than a one-time errand boy, Dr Duhig, then, and I think still, Roman Catholic Archbishop of Brisbane. Taking one thing with another, I was doing just as well as if I had a regular job as a reporter and I was having a far more interesting time.

The historian priest paid without a murmur the stiff bill I sent him when the devilling was completed, and I began to look around for a permanent position on a paper.

Wherever I tried, I met with an even more friendly reception than that accorded me in Sydney. The most imposing-looking of the Brisbane newspaper establishments I left to the last. Eventually I screwed up courage and asked to see the managing editor. Within two minutes I was seated in an armchair opposite him, smoking his cigarette and drinking his coffee, while he, apologising for inability to attend to me for some time, was busy examining a layout plan that had been put before him for his approval.

'Now then,' he said, turning to me, when he had finished with the plan, 'you're looking for a job, eh? No crime in that. We've all had to do it some time or other. Where do you come from? Kimberley!' he repeated. 'It's the devil of a distance to come all the way round from West Australia for a job. What's that? Kimberley, South Africa! How many bloody thousand miles is that? Well, you deserve a job after all that travelling for one. We must simply find you one. I'll call in our staff editor.'

To the staff editor he introduced me as the latest thing in marvels to have, as he Australianised it, 'lobbed' into Brisbane. A job must be found for me. The staff bloke was not quite so enthusiastic. If I had but come a fortnight earlier, all might have been well. There had been a vacancy then. But Mr Wright must remember that vacancy had been filled. If I'd call again in six weeks, all would certainly be well. One of the senior reporters would then be going down to Melbourne to cover the Federal Parliamentary session. I could have a temporary job for three months. In those three months probably I could be fitted in permanently.

'Six weeks!' roared the manager. 'Damn it! The man's got to

live in those six weeks. You're not the least bit of use. Send me Mr Dunn.'

Mr Dunn, he explained to me, was the head of the proofreading department. Could I read proofs? I assured him I had read miles of proofs. But I did not explain to him the somewhat archaic conditions under which I had read them; one eye on the copy and one on the proof. One of Mr Dunn's readers had gone sick the previous day and would likely be laid up for a couple of months. Mr Dunn would fix me up.

Mr Dunn, a greying, floridly-faced old gentleman, scraggily bearded, let it be known that his department was the most important on the paper. He wanted none but tried men and true in it. It was true, he admitted, that one of his readers would be away for a long time, but he would prefer to distribute the work among proven readers to taking on a stranger temporarily. Dunn, I gathered from the manager's way of speaking to him, was a man to be humoured in his whimsies. The manager reminded him that he was a great churchgoer. Then he ought to be ready to do a work of mercy by enabling the hungry to feed themselves. At length Dunn, a bit grudgingly, assented to putting me on trial for the night. Pay was 12/6 per night.

At eight that evening I entered the proofreading room. I sat down by my copy-holder, a being hitherto unheard of by me, who was a just-left-school youth with adenoids and droned the copy into my ears, calling out the minutiae of punctuation after the way of 'Stainless Stephen', but without that comedian's sparkle, while my pen raced along the damp galley proof.

After about half an hour I got the hang of the game. I learned to cut myself off, as it were, from the din caused by thirty other adenoidal youngsters similarly reading out copy to other proofreaders. At smoke-o (Australian for breaktime) Dunn padded along to me.

'You're doing very well,' said he. 'I can make a good reader out of any man or woman who can spot sixty per cent of the mistakes after a week. You're getting eighty per cent of them first time. That's remarkably good.'

Thus cheered, I resumed and towards morning covered myself with glory in his eyes. A sub-editor in expanding an English cable had perpetrated some schoolboy howlers in history. In the 'last revise', a good many of which, I noticed, were now being passed on to me, I detected the blunders. In Dunn's estimation was I greatly exalted. I had saved the paper from ridicule. I have since wondered what trouble I stirred up for the sub-editor who didn't know his history.

I had a fortnight as proofreader. The pay was very welcome in its way, but I disliked the job. It was noisy and productive of headaches. I had always detested night work even in the fire station in Kimberley where one could sleep enough at night if one could jump up wide awake at the first boom of the fire alarm or at the first tinkle of the telephone bell. And in the heat of a Brisbane day one could get very little sleep, especially in the boarding-house of Mrs Perry where there was always the clatter and chatter of cooking meals or of eating them.

As I sat on the veranda of the boarding-house one Friday afternoon, I was surprised to see Mr Dunn padding up the hill street towards it. He walked so heavily on his heels that one expected to see him fall backwards. He sat down with me and unfolded the reason for his coming to see me.

One of the regular readers had resigned that morning. Nothing would please him more than that I should take over the vacant chair. The pay would be quite a bit better than that I could get as a junior reporter, and he would see that by delegating to me some of his own supervisory duties I would be well in line to take over his place when in a couple of years he would retire.

I liked the old man. He was, it is true, a 'wowser', Australianese for killjoy, but he was a decidedly likeable specimen of that class. While he was urging me to accept, a postman came in and handed me a letter I had ceased hoping to get. Some weeks before I had answered an advertisement stating that a reporter was wanted on a high-class country paper. My application had been accepted and I was to report immediately for work. I passed the letter across to Dunn as my answer to him. I told him I felt that reporting was much more to my liking than was proofreading. There was just a tinge of bitterness in his farewell to me.

The most immediately I could report to the country paper was by midday on the Saturday. I wired it to that effect and exactly at noon on the Saturday I stalked into its office in a town that called itself the inland capital of Queensland and was by far the largest town of a district famous for farming and dairy produce and larger than the whole of Britain. I asked to see the managing director, who had signed the letter notifying me of my appointment.

'I'm that bloke,' replied a stubbily bearded, rotund man, ambling over to the counter. 'Are you our new reporter? Well, what the hell hurry are you in? We didn't expect you till the end of next week at the earliest. We don't work here on Saturdays, so there's nobody about. Ever been in this town before? No. Well, go and have a good look round it. Stroll round here about eight o'clock tomorrow night. The rest of the boys will be in then, and I'll take you round and introduce you to the "family". Come along now and have a drink, and, by the way, your pay starts from this minute.'

I found Toowoomba rather depressing on a wet Saturday and on a wet Sunday and the boarding-house into which I had been inveigled by a 'runner' when the train from Brisbane had pulled up in the station a trifle more than depressing. The only other boarder in it was an elderly chap in from the bush and, it seemed to me, in his pursuit of the bushman's ideal state when in town: not 'seeing daylight' and fast working himself towards the DTs.

At eight o'clock on the Sunday night I was at the office of the *Toowoomba Chronicle*. This time there were two directors to welcome me, each an almost exact replica of the other except that the stubby brown beard of the man I had first met was replaced by a white one in the second. They took me upstairs and introduced me to the editor, the sub-editor, the reporter on night-shift, and in a procession we all went into the machine room where six Linotypes were clattering away. There I was introduced to the operators, the stone-hand, as they called him, the engineer, the grinning printer's devil and two or three others whose jobs on the paper did not seem to have distinctive appellations. Beer was sent out for; speeches were made welcoming me to the 'family' and assuring me that all of them would do their damnedest to make my time with them a happy time. As more than half those in the machine room had Irish names, I judged that my time with them would not be without its moments of interest. Then I was bidden get off to bed and have a good night's rest so that I might be fresh for day duty on the Monday.

I have had since then more than thirty years in which to listen to criticism by English folk of the Australians. Many of these criticisms, especially round about 1932–33 were uninformed and bitter. Is it any wonder I often find myself looking back with very kindly memories to the days when I was in:

'The land of lots of time
And the kind Australian ways?'

10

The paper had been started some seventy years before, I was told, by a Devonshire man, who must have imparted to it in very great measure the family atmosphere it still retained in 1914.

Whether he died intestate or not I never found out, but the paper passed on his death to the entire family of five sons and two daughters. Three of the sons were under various titles then actively engaged in the management of it. Mr John was managing director. Mr Fred carried out an Olympian supervision of accounts and Mr Harry had a similar detached post in charge of sales and advertisements. Another brother, Mr Tom, a lawyer with, I gathered, a very fine practice, showed up every evening in the office and scribbled assiduously for a couple of hours. He was our racing expert, and, as with all such experts, his tips occasionally came off. The fifth brother we rarely saw, as he spent most of his time in Melbourne in federal politics. And we had but very rare glimpses of the Misses Harriet and Janet, still referred to and addressed as 'Misses', though they were by this time married and rather matronly in appearance. The firm could boast that no employee had ever left or been discharged from its employment, that lads joining it as messengers stayed on to become qualified in some branch of the trade. As a matter of fact, the lad who was the ink-bespattered printer's devil in 1914 was, when I met him in London in 1919 as an Australian soldier, a recognised Linotype operator.

Reporting in this Queensland town was vastly more difficult than had been reporting in South Africa. There was a great deal more of it for one thing, as there were meetings of all sorts of councils and boards, sometimes as many as three or four a day. There were but three of us to cover all these. For a time I found this a strain as I never was anything near a verbatim reporter. But I got round my lack of speed by listening to Councillor Bigwind, and Mr Talltalk, making occasional notes of what they were trying to say and then putting in my reports as if they had said it. This trick pleased them immensely. Some of them would request that I be sent to 'cover' meetings at which they intended to orate. They never spoke so well they said, as when I reported them. One had alternate weeks of day- and night-shift, and when one was on night-shift, one had to do the most of the sub-editing. It was rather jolly being on night-shift in a way. At smoke-o we all toddled about together in the machine room, eating our sandwiches, drinking our coffee or beer. Most of us drank beer. About half an hour before smoke-o the printer's devil went the rounds of all the staff collecting 'kicks' and 'half-kicks', otherwise shillings and sixpences, and then slipped out the back way to a pub and brought back the beer in a can of several gallons capacity, shared it out among us according to the amount we had contributed. And at times one of our Mrs would march the lot of us to the pub by this backyard route and prolong the break from ten minutes to half an hour. Then there was general celebration during which we assured ourselves that we were the staff of the finest country paper in Queensland. And so I think we were: certainly *The Chronicle* was well ahead of any other country sheets I saw in Queensland and for that matter ahead of country papers I saw from the other states. And if there had been an exciting night in putting our paper to bed, a well-attended pilgrimage to the pub even at 3 a.m. was the recognised routine. Whatever the hour, the publican was ever ready to admit us. The editor, being, as surprisingly large numbers of Australians are, a strict teetotaller, never came with us on these jaunts and jollities, but hurried home to his invalid wife. Though he was a wowser, Bill Hargett was much respected by all of us.

The sub-editor, young Mr Lit, was also senior reporter and marked out to be the editor one day. Poor lad, he never reached that eminence for he laid down the red wine of his youth in the mud of Passchendaele. He was rather light-hearted and responsibility sat lightly on him. The other reporter was a rosy-faced English youth known to all except the editor as 'Stew'. By the editor he was addressed as Mr Bainton. He had got his name some time when in search of local news he had visited a camp of Commonwealth Military Forces on the outskirts of the town. He had listened to the moans of the privates about the quality of their stew. All the blame had been laid on the cooks. He had gone back to the office and written up some very scathing lines on the stew. Going back in a couple of days to find whether his article had had any effect, he discovered it had. It had enraged the cooks, who pursued him with axes and cleavers out of the camp, threatening to chop him up and put the bits of him into the stew. So 'Stew' he became to his colleagues. He was an excellent and very fast writer of shorthand, in whom in some of my own difficulties with that art I found a very helpful friend.

The part of the work at which I was happiest was the sub-editing. Here the wide reading I had done in South Africa was of very great help to me. My knowledge ranged over big fields of geography, history, current affairs and the like. Thus what in a cable from England or a wire from Australia was often Greek or worse to Mr Lit and 'Stew' was as clear as day to me. Besides, there was a very fine reference library in the editor's room, and I soon learned to consult it on points on which I was in doubt. The other two scorned the taking of such pains. As used to be said in the monastery, they went mostly on the 'dabitur', i.e. on the inspiration of the moment. That often led them into making ridiculous mistakes such as inserting in a cable that a river mentioned therein was in Africa whereas it was in America or that a town with a romantic name was in South America. They talked lightly of having made such blunders and recounted an incident during the Balkan War. When news was short and, as sometimes happened as the result of such a shortage, there were some square inches of the paper to be filled up, the easiest way to do this was to shove in a war map. One night the call for more 'copy' rang out, and they had recourse to the war map. Lit dived to the cupboard in which the blocks for such maps were kept, did not glance at the one he picked up for he thought that the block of the map of the Balkans, being the most in use, would be the one on top. Unfortunately somebody else had during the day been rummaging in the cupboard. The block he picked up was one of Mexico. Lit laughed very heartily over having illustrated the Balkan War by a map of Mexico. 'What's the odds?' he demanded. 'Of course, it gets the dads' hackles up, but look what a number of damned fools write in or come in to tell us we were wrong! Things like that keep up interest in the paper.'

However, one night, with all my knowledge and all my research, I was beaten by finding two words occurring in a rather long cable from London which gave the tumultuous outpouring of some politician of those days. 'Carbine ob.' were the two words. Of course, the *ob.* was an old one among sub-editors; it was merely a contraction of the Latin *obit* meaning deceased. I could not think or find out what a carbine dying could refer to. I cut out the words and in a quiet moment took them into Bill Hargett to see whether he could throw any light on the mystery. As soon as he saw them, Bill lost for once his usual calm. 'Ring up Mr Tom at once,' he bade me. 'Send young Harry [one of the messengers, the beer fetcher] round to the cab rank and tell him to send a cab up Mr Tom's residence and fetch him here. Harry's to run like ——, as fast as he can,' he amended, 'and get Mr Tom here as soon as possible. Then get Bill Heany to clear his machine. The make-up man is to throw out two or three columns. This is most important. All Australia will get worked up over it.'

Mr Tom presently arrived, sat down and began consulting some racing books. 'Carbine,' it transpired, had been a famous Australian racehorse, which had been sold to an English racing syndicate for stud purposes. Next morning *The Chronicle* had three columns with many crossheadings telling all about the horse's famous career. It was something of a scoop. The other subs had evidently been

CIVIL SERVICE ASSOCIATION FOOTBALL CLUB.
WINNERS SECOND LEAGUE, KIMBERLEY, 1909.

Above:
Captain of the team
(with ball).
Kimberley 1909

Left:
Anzac Days.
Captain Peter Murphy
MBE, 1919.

Left:
Bride to be,
Ethel Gillings.

Below:
Later years.
Peter and Ethel at
Dornton Road SW12.

Above:
Three Australians on York House roof, Cairo. They broke camp for three days and apparently enjoyed themselves!

Left:
Final resting place. Streatham Cemetery

Below:
On Carnally Rocks. Pat (first cousin), Peter (son) and Sean (grandson), 1998.

IN
LOVING MEMORY OF
Capt.
PETER KEVIN MURPHY M.B.E.
BORN 8 OCT. 1881
DIED 5 MAY 1954
HIS WIFE
ETHEL MARIE MURPHY
BORN 30 JAN. 1894
DIED 26 DEC. 1979

R.I.P.

28920.22

Fortis Et Hospitalis

The Murphy of Carnally "Clan"

Commemorating

The Grand Gathering

19th ~ 20th July 2002

O! The hills around Carnally
They come surging through my dreams
I see Carnally's barren rocks
Its bushes and its streams.

(Pete Murphy 1881-1954)

Above:
Grand Gathering.

unable or had not bothered, to spot any significance in 'Carbine ob.'

The night was generally a pretty hectic time for work. One might have been at a meeting from eight to ten and would therefore have a longish report of one's own to lick into shape before settling down to the subbing. Then about midnight late news was phoned through to us from an agency on the coast. These phone messages had to be taken down in shorthand, transcribed and sent out to the compositors. And as there would usually be about twelve country papers linked up with the agency and twelve reporters imploring the agency man to speak his message slowly, to repeat parts of it, to explain what the hell he meant by some of the words he was broadcasting, the taking down of the message was not easy for a fellow who could jot down shorthand at a much faster rate than I could. And the man on night duty had to read all the proofs after the manner to which I had been accustomed in Kimberley: one eye on the copy, the other on the still damp proof. Still, there was such an atmosphere of good fellowship about *The Chronicle* that the hardest work on it partook of something of the nature of pleasure.

I had moved from the temperance hotel to which I had gone the first day I struck Toowoomba. That hotel was rather a sordid place. The rooms were small, nothing much more than hutches. It was right up against the railway station, and the chug-chugging of goods trains and shunting engines kept one awake most of the night. In addition to this I proved quite right in my forecast about the bushman. He cut his throat one morning and made rather a mess of the job. In the dining-room sat the poor old devil with his neck heavily bandaged, his face as wan as a wax candle, and pools of blood were soaking into the linoleum around his feet. That evening in the office I sought the advice of our advertisement canvasser as to a place in which to lodge, in which there would be a bit more comfort generally and in which suicidal attempts would not be likely. I should try the Tara Hotel, he told me. It was kept, he informed me, by an Irishwoman married to an Austrian: but old Hans was all right. It would not be easy to get into it, for Mrs Strohfield was mighty particular about her boarders.

I went along to the Tara to make enquiries. 'No,' said the big, blond, bearded man behind the bar as I was sipping the whisky and soda meant to oil my approach. 'No, son, you can't come here. The wife won't be bothered with boarders. Too much trouble they are. We've got only two, and they're friends of ours. What's that? You're Irish, are you? Now, that's different altogether. I wouldn't say but she'd take you. She's out at the theatre this evening. Call again in the morning and you can put "the hard word" on her then.'

In the morning I met a massive woman, whose colleen face, blue eyes and black hair still spoke of the dew on Meath meadows.

'Well, now, glory be to God; shure it's welcome you'll be. There's about twenty empty rooms upstairs. Run up an' have a look at them. Pick the one that suits ye best. I'm a bit fat to be stravaig up with ye.

'What terms is it? Would a pound a week be too much for ye? That's with four good meals a day an' yer wee bit o' washin' thrown in an' a cup o'tay any time ye want it. Too chape, ye say? Well, we've made as much money as'll do us for our day an' we can't be takin any iv it wid us. So that's all right. I didn't axe ye if you were a Catholic, but wid a name like yours ye would be. Now, I hope you go to Mass an' yer duties regularly. If ye don't, out ye'll go. "*Maith go brath leath*" if ye know what that manes. Shure come in as soon as ye like. I won't be chargin' ye anything till ye do come in.'

I wasn't very long about coming in. I met the other two boarders in this uniquely run hotel. One was Bill Cody, Irish-Australian; the other Jem Doyle, a Kilkenny boy, teacher in an elementary school in Toowoomba, and soon to end his life at twenty-three in the Flanders mud. Bill was middle-aged, with spare sandy hair much streaked with grey. He carried on some kind of a provision agency, spending his days as a delivery salesman driving out to the villages and hamlets about the town. Sometimes he drove his own horses, of which he had three, but mostly the animals he drove were those he was training for wealthy people in the neighbourhood. Often he would take me with him on his rounds if through being on night-shift I had the afternoon free. Always on Sundays he took Doyle and myself with him on runs out to some of the beauty spots round Toowoomba. There were many of these, the most notable being 'The Range', a long ridge of the East Australian range about a mile distant from the centre of the town. On a clear Sunday afternoon a visit to 'The Range' was a great pleasure. From the top of the ridge one could see fold after fold of the wooded mountains stretching away eastwards as still and motionless as if the folds were waves of the sea frozen into immobility at the height of the storm by the breath of the Almighty. And beyond the folds one could see a rim of blue, which might be the meeting of sky and earth or might be the sea and sky. Bill was a fine raconteur and would ever be telling us of his various experiences in his search for fortune in all the outlandish parts of Australia. He had been in on the early discoveries of gold in Western Australia and had nearly died of thirst on the trail to Kalgoorlie.

Life went in great jollity in the Tara. Apart from the bar, which was mostly served by Hans and his son-in-law, there was a household staff of two: one was Molly Gill, the niece of Mrs Strohfield; the other a niece to Hans. Molly was a buxom lass of about twenty-five, laughing, joking and full of all kinds of devilment such as making apple-pie beds and even sewing up the bed sheets when we annoyed her. The Austrian girl was a good deal older than Molly. She too was prone to larks, but set about them with more seriousness of mien than did the ever-laughing Irish lass. Molly was the housemaid, and Gussie was the cook.

So, in this very pleasant atmosphere, both in *The Chronicle* office and in the Tara, things ran on until the end of July. Nobody recognised that the faint cloud that blew up in the Balkans at the beginning of that month was going to blow up into a storm that would put life in a bit of a muddle for the lot of us.

Just as July was drawing to a close the floodgates of Australian political oratory were thrown open by the announcement of a federal general election. This meant that the reporters were out every night taking down the prattlings of the Australian tweedledums and tweedledees, a task which I found very boring.

It must have been on the last Saturday of July that Bill Hargett and I, on the way to and from a Rugby international at Brisbane between New Zealand and Australia, were chatting about the Austrian ultimatum to Serbia. Bill was very pessimistic over it. 'It'll shatter the world,' said he. 'We'll feel the crash even here in Queensland.' I laughed. Within a fortnight it was to end my brief career as a newspaper reporter.

11

On the day following England's entry into the war the bickering Australian politicians declared a truce in their abusively wordy battles with one another and united in their agreement that England should have Australia's last man and last shilling. Australians, remembering the mighty deeds of Australians in the Boer War, wished the politicians meant it all. When I got to the office that evening I got news that I did not greatly like. I was, the managing director informed me, to remain on night duty for the duration of the war so that I could always take a hand in the sub-editing of the war news.

Then one morning about ten days after England's declaration of war I could not get to sleep. Hans had made an early start on some home carpentry, which appeared to involve much driving of nails into very hard wood. Two of his grandchildren were galloping about on the veranda. Even fairy footsteps on that veranda would resound like drum beats.

I got up and went for a walk, hoping that the hotel would be a bit more peaceful in the afternoon. In my walk I happened to pass the Toowoomba drill hall. It had already been decreed that Australia was to send an expedition overseas, and from the front of the hall a banner announced that my king and country needed me. What with the want of sleep and a slight quarrel with friend Doyle on the previous evening, I was in somewhat of a depressed mood. So far I had not thought of joining up, though I had occasionally been feeling that it would be a fine thing to be helping France and be one with the Sarsfields, Dillons and O'Briens of the one-time Irish Brigade of, '*semper et ubique fidelis*' (always and everywhere faithful).

I pulled out a coin and tossed it. 'Heads, I go: tails, I don't.' It came down heads. I went in and to a rather supercilious officer behind a desk announced that here was I, sound in mind and limb, a candidate for the force that Australia was enrolling for overseas service.

He gave me a look, which said very plainly that he thought Australia could get on very well without me. His questions emphasised that look. Had I ever been in any army? Had I been a member of any territorial or volunteer force? Had I ever been a member of a rifle club? Had I ever had a rifle in my hand?

He listened to my succession of negatives, then said I had no chance whatever, but supposed he might as well add my name to the already long list in front of him. He took down my age and address and added the equivalent of 'I won't be seeing you.'

I reckoned I'd never hear anything more of it. I went on listening of an evening to tweedledum abusing tweedledee, got back to the office to fit up a report of their mouthings, dealt with cables from London and prayed that the war would soon be over that I might be released from this maddening torture of continual night-shift.

In a few days, however, I had a notification that I was to present myself at the drill hall on a certain night, on which a selection would be made of those who would constitute Australia's first contingent for overseas service. That night about seven, Bill Hargett gave us our assignments for the evening. 'Mr Murphy! You run along to the drill hall. There's something going on there about the selection of the contribution that Toowoomba and district is to make to the Queensland battalion for service abroad. Give it about a couple of "sticks".' I held out to him my notification from the military authorities that I was already booked for attendance thereat. 'Oh, that!' said Bill. 'Doesn't mean a thing. From what I hear, not one in twenty of those who have volunteered will be picked. There are only thirty men being picked from here. There are far more than enough old soldiers and Commonwealth

Military Forces – you know, the Saturday afternoon warriors – kicking around to make up that number.'

To no one else had I mentioned my having volunteered. When I next met Bill, I was Private P.K. Murphy of the Australian Imperial Force. There were upwards of six hundred of us volunteers jammed in the drill hall that Wednesday evening. In and out among us, full of their own importance, trotted about a large number of the youthful Australian Militia, nearly all showing their stripes and showing us that they regarded us as not much better than dust the wind had blown in off the street. And like dust we ourselves felt when ordered to strip to have our measurements taken before being medically examined. At the measurement business I caused something of a sensation. All my rigorous South African training for football and long-distance running had given me what was looked upon as the phenomenal chest expansion of twelve inches. Twice I shot the measuring tape out of an officer's fingers. Height: five feet eleven. The doctor proclaimed me as an extraordinarily healthy animal, and the major, who was to take charge of the Toowoomba selection, bundled me at once into the chosen thirty on the grounds that I would be likely to stop twice as many bullets as would anybody else. Warned to present myself next day for attestation and to be at the hall again on the Saturday morning at 6.30 ready to entrain for camp, I got back to the office just as the smoke-o there was starting. There was a pile of London press messages awaiting my attention, and Lit, who was in charge that night, 'roused' me for being late, so holding up the night's work. I handed him my travel order for the training camp outside Brisbane. After a few gasps of astonishment and a profanely worded prayer of pity for me when he heard what I had done he went whooping into the machine room, bawdily chanting of what the nation got and what the soldier got when he was marching to the front. Many journeys through the backyard made the beer can that night, and the printer's devil, Bainton and myself were the only sober members of the night staff when the paper went to bed. We broke up the party at 5 a.m.

Mr John, when I timidly entered the office in the late afternoon, took me aside, told me that he was intensely proud of the fine example I had set the whole of the newspaper profession of Australia, proud beyond measure of *The Chronicle's* association with me, and assured me that, were the duration of the war long or short, my job would be kept open for me. For the rest of the time I was a civilian I was to regard myself as on holiday, but was to be at the office at eight on the Friday night in order that the 'family' could bid me farewell. That they did right nobly with champagne and a wristlet watch, to whose uncertain going the plunge into the sea at the Gallipoli landing would later put an end.

For the two days before we went to camp we were feted, photographed and had our capacities for absorbing drink fully tested. Just after dawn on the Saturday morning, August 19th, I think it was, the selected thirty assembled outside the drill hall. A damp, chill mist made us feel that heroism has its depressing moments. We were pushed around by the babyfaced NCOs of the Commonwealth Forces. Shivering, we were photographed, shoved into, rather than formed, fours, about turned, falling over our feet and banging our heads together. 'Quick march!' roared the major. The band struck up 'The Girl I Left Behind Me', and we started on what we said was to be our march to Berlin.

Toowoomba was astir by now; the sun was breaking in golden hues through the mist; a breeze was fluttering the flags which decorated every building. The pavements were thronged; women in all stages of negligée crowded the windows and the doorways of the houses. Thunderous was the cheering as, with long steps, short steps and little hope to get the step, we swung through the town, heads held high, and chests stuck out. Near the station the enthusiasm broke into madness. The 'family' was there in full force. It pulled me from such rank as we had been able to keep. Minus a shoe, thrown in after me, I was tossed into the train through an open carriage window. Men, women and children fought their way to the train windows to kiss us. To a deafening crackle of detonators and the roaring of the crowd the train pulled out of the station.

'God in Heaven!' cried a sergeant-major, surveying us very critically when in the afternoon, howling our own versions of 'Rule Britannia' and the like, we reached camp headquarters, 'am I expected to make soldiers out of b——y dingoes like you? Get over there, you flat-footed, knock-kneed, lopsided, spavined lot of gravel crushers! Lie down and keep the grass from growing. That's about all you'll ever be good for.'

A few more eulogies of that sort during the evening took much of the elation out of us. Heroism seemed a peculiarly uncomfortable business that night as we expressed astonishment that what seemed be soft Queensland grass should conceal so many bumps unfriendly to our bodies. On the Sunday morning as we sat sorrowfully about in that grass trying to drink tea that, sugarless and milkless, tasted as if it were burnt water, and trying to chew lumps of steak that, burnt on the outside, were raw within, I'd have liked to be back in the Tara Hotel within sound of the soft teasing voice of Molly Gill and perhaps the pinch of her fingers on my ear as she put the customary heaped plate of bacon and eggs in front of me.

In a couple of days I dropped on what promised to be a very cushy job. As we were scrambling about to get ready for the forenoon parade, word came round that the colonel wanted a secretary. 'Private Murphy,' said our captain, 'you've been a newspaper reporter. Fall out and report at the colonel's tent.'

I went along and sat on the grass outside the colonel's tent till the old man, trying to make the steps of age look like the springings of youth, came along from telling his company officers to carry on.

'Come inside, my man,' said he. 'Sit down on the major's bed, my boy. We've got a lot of work to get through. How about a drink before we start?'

I had no objection. We lowered liberal tots of whisky. We got thirsty talking of the fighting somewhere ahead of us and lowered a couple more. Then he dictated three brief letters to me and solicitously enquired whether I could have them ready for his signature by 6 p.m. I thought I could just about manage that much. On no account, he enjoined, was I to do anything else but his letters. He then went off to Brisbane, and I went off to have a crack at the orderly room typewriter.

For a week I got along very nicely with morning whiskies to aid me through the stiff task of typing three or four letters a day. This seemed to me a splendid sort of warfare. Then the old man was rather pointedly informed that the war establishment for a battalion of infantry did not allow for a secretary for the colonel. The adjutant told me I'd have to be an orderly room clerk reporting for duty at 7 a.m. and remaining on duty till 8 p.m. In these thirteen hours, if there was nothing else to be done, I might type what private letters I liked for the colonel or anybody else, but I'd have to take my full share in the general clerical work of the orderly room.

A whole day in the orderly room did not appeal to me as any sort of fun, particularly as when training was over at 4 p.m. my mates of the battalion were free to go into Brisbane. After two days of it I took my rifle and went with it to the parade ground, where I became the most awkward member of the awkward squad and suffered accordingly from the tongue of a British sergeant-major. Still, within a month he had us so licked into shape that we could manage quite decently to perform all the elementary movements of our drill. And that the Australians were desperately keen to learn.

We had our first big grievance over our company officers. We thought we should have some say in deciding who should be in command of us. At the start we had as our lieutenant a bright, laughing Brisbane youth, whom we almost adored. When he was taken from us to be put in charge of the battalion machine-gun section, at first we did not like the bow-legged, black-moustached man with hair showing streaks of grey put in charge of us. But for this bantam Geordie – in civilian life a fitter in the Queensland

Railway workshops – every man of us would soon have willingly laid down life. He won complete ascendency from us, did this Jock Roberts.

The NCOs were a sore trial to us. They were mostly ex-regulars of the British Army, bullying, blustering, unpicturesquely foul of speech, working out on us the tradition of abuse from which they, themselves, suffered on the barrack square. The other NCOs, mostly 'kids' of the Commonwealth Forces, unable to carry off the bullying and the blustering, had recourse to a biting sarcasm, which was still harder to endure. But blustering, bullying and sarcasm alike lost point against the affectation of stupidity or innocence the Australians could so easily put up. A bellowing English sergeant was completely nonplussed by an Australian saying to him, 'Beg your pardon, sarge! Would you mind just speaking up a little? I'm a bit hard of hearing, you see.' And when our CMF colour-sergeant sent a party of us wood chopping for the cooks' fires at a time when we thought we were entitled to be taking part in a charge on the wet canteen, he came after us to find out why we were not getting on with the job. He found the whole lot of us intently studying the blade and handles of the axes. We were, we told him, looking for instructions as to the use of the tools.

About the middle of that September rumours began to circulate amongst us that we were to be moved off for action. We were being vaccinated, inoculated, foot-inspected, teeth-inspected and, bigger shock to some of us, short-arm inspected. And this time the 'furfy', as the Australians called such rumours, proved true.

On September 23rd we got the order to get ready to move out. No hint of where we were moving to. That was a day of great shouting, of instruction and counter-instruction. The dear old colonel assembled us and lectured to us in the tones of one who was leading a crusade. Especially did he warn us against the risks of contracting venereal disease. That would be the highest betrayal of the sacred cause on which we were engaged. Those who contracted such a disease in even its mildest form would be expelled from the battalion, branded with disgrace and returned in ignominy to Australia.

There came with the cessation of the day's furies our last night on Queensland soil. Tents had been struck, and the battalion was 'bushing' it beneath the 'wondrous glory of the everlasting stars', as a bush poet has it. And as the stars paled before the oncoming dawn, we were marching to the station in the utmost silence. No singing, no shouting. The enemy, we were warned, might hear of our movement.

The train rumbled about a sleeping Brisbane and pulled up at Bulimba Dock, along which, very indistinct of outline, lay a mail boat, the *Omrah*, converted into a trooper. An hour later in the misty spreading daylight she moved down the river. A few of us, leaning against the bulwarks, were looking back on the quiet city and voicing our anticipation of the day when, triumphant, the battalion would yet again march through the beflagged streets of Brisbane. With a 'Hello, boys! At last we're off' our company captain, a lecturer on history at some Australian university, whom we held in high regard, perhaps because he could mix the most lurid abuse with smiles, joined us and listened to these anticipations. He laughed.

'Something called the Ninth Battalion may march again through the Brisbane streets, but very few of you will be in it.'

'Well, who will, skipper?' he was asked.

'Its 85th reinforcements, I guess,' he answered.

That took a lot of the light-heartedness from us. And it proved a not inaccurate forecast. By November, 1918, I was told, there were but a dozen or so of those who sailed out among the jellyfish that September morn still serving with the battalion. Not all the missing had been killed. Some of them had been invalided out of it because of wounds. Some more, like myself, declared unfit for active service, were still serving in base units of the Australian Imperial Force.

12

For the four days it took us to reach Melbourne the ship rolled and pitched, as did the insides of the warriors, most of whom were having their first experience of life on the ocean wave. The hardened wanderers of the world among us looked on superiorly, taunting their brethren of weaker stomachs by remarks about the dietetic advantages of fat pork.

Tied up to a dockside, we lay in Port Melbourne for nearly a month. By day we went ashore, making dreary marches through dockside slums to a region of sand-dunes along the bay. Among these dunes we'd practise fighting as laid down in 1914, firing imaginary rounds at imaginary enemies, jumping up and rushing imaginary enemy positions. The positions were always captured, of course, and then our sergeants would lecture on how well or how badly we had done the job. If they had been rough of tongue on us during the skirmishing, most of us would be lying about on the sand behind them, yelling that we were casualties and roaring for the 'tar bucket' or for 'Gertie' and his stretcher bearers. 'Gertie' was our MO. What he had done to deserve such a name I do not know. He had been an Oxford cross-country runner in his youth and was even now in his fifties about as tough as teak.

We had by this time worked up several grievances: one about pay, of which we could draw only a bob a day while on the ship (and we did not consider that Fort Melbourne was the High Seas); and another that there was no wet canteen on board for NCOs and other ranks, though the officers could get as much booze as they liked (and some of them were obviously getting a lot more than was good for them). Nothing so maddened the Australians as discrimination in the way of privilege. The third, and perhaps the biggest, outcry was about our pets. We had accumulated quite a variety of these: a kangaroo, a couple of dogs of very mixed ancestry, one of them an Australian cattle-dog as far as any breed was recognisable in it. But they had been acquired entirely unofficially and so had to be left behind before our departure from Australia. The only animal we were allowed to take was a bull-terrier, which to the majority of us had nothing distinctive of Australia about it and was rather disliked by most of us as the brute had an uncertain temper. He afterwards became quite famous on Gallipoli as 'Buller' and was, I think, ultimately presented to the British Navy in gratitude for the support which that arm had rendered the Australians.

All grumbles died away as one sunny afternoon in late October the *Omrah* headed down Port Philip Bay for the open sea. We cheered, we sang and played about like released schoolboys. Weren't we Queenslanders the first Australians to be moving off to the Great War?

Five days later, having crossed the Bight in good weather we found ourselves just after dawn creeping in through winding inlets fronted by great bare rocks that stood as sentinels over the waters. Away in front of us snugged up in a fold of the hills was a little town, on which the rising sun was weaving patterns of light and shade. In these inlets, we were informed, we were to rendezvous with the ships taking the Australian and New Zealand divisions to Europe, as we thought. That ours was that morning the only boat on those wide expanses of water gave us occasion for great pride in ourselves.

Daily other boats came into the inlets, and pride of an empire would bubble up within us of an evening we would look out over the network of masts and riggings. Such a sight of shipping for such a purpose had never before been seen.

Soon after daybreak on November 1st, the *Omrah* leading, the ships started moving out for the ocean. The sky was without a speck of cloud; the West Australian hills were golden in the light of the rising sun. The dried-up watercourses on the slopes of these hills were as streaks of silver; the sentinel rocks gleamed like walls of quartz. Many of us were looking our last on Australia.

When on the open sea the ships took up formation, there were forty-two transports in the convoy. In addition there were our escorting war vessels, Australian and Japanese cruisers and a Canadian Pacific liner converted to war purposes.

We were getting daily in closer touch with our sergeants. By this time they had come to realise that their chances of turning us into submissive infantry on the British model were very slight. They began to play down to us. Part of the time they had us on deck for lectures on infantry tactics, but they would usually talk to us of things far more interesting to us. They and we now supposed that we were bound for England. One of them was one day talking to us of the tactics to be adopted if we found ourselves involved in arguments in English pubs.

'Don't argue with any bastard,' urged the sergeant. 'You just grab a bottle and bring it down on his head.'

The door behind him opened just then and out stepped our lecturer on history.

'Begging your pardon, sir,' said the sergeant, 'isn't that right, sir? When you're so close to your enemy that you haven't room to use your bayonet, the best thing to do is to up with the butt of your rifle and bring it down on the head?'

'Not quite, sergeant,' replied the captain without the flicker of a smile. 'In the circumstances the best thing to do would be to up with your boot and give him a kick in the belly.'

Another was similarly interrupted in a talk on what the bearing of a good Australian should be among the lassies of Leicester Square.

'What are you dealing with now, sergeant?' asked the officer.

'Just been explaining to them, sir, some points about the correct treatment of civilians in the sphere of operations. Shall I run through them again, sir?'

We worked up new acts of grievances, this time mainly about the stuffiness of our quarters and a further cutting of our 'draw', which was now to be only 10/- a fortnight, and even that after a sort of means test, which we all passed successfully. At six o'clock every evening the portholes were screwed up tight by a member of the crew. When brought on deck of an evening, as we sometimes were, the striking of a match was forbidden. And what was an Australian good for unless he had a fag on? We'd like to know. Being treated like old women we were or like kids on a Sunday school picnic!

When we were drawing nigh Colombo we were told that the reason for restrictions on light was the presence somewhere in these waters of the German raider, the *Emden*, which, if opportunity offered, was pretty certain to attack the convoy and possibly send a couple of transports to the bottom. We took our nightly gloom and want of air a little bit more placidly thereafter, and one afternoon we noticed unusual activity among the escorting war vessels. For a few minutes they buzzed about like mosquitoes. Then thick banks of smoke curled up from one of them. She veered around losing all outline in a trail of smoke and hared off towards the horizon on what was manifestly an errand of frenzied haste. We sought the reason for this haste, but it was only next afternoon we found it when it was announced to us that the Australian cruiser *Sydney* had caught the *Emden* off the Cocos Islands while she was destroying the cable station there and had put an end to her raiding.

Another outburst of discontent off Colombo, at the refusal of leave, died away when it was announced that about fifty of the *Emden's* prisoners would be put on our boat for us to guard them thence to Suez, where they would be handed over to a British battleship for ultimate disposal. There was great competition to be a member of the guard, for those composing it would be relieved of all the boring 'spasms' that had hitherto made our time at sea a trial. One hundred of the smartest looking and best conducted men of the battalion were to be chosen for this guard duty. We were to be very firm with the prisoners, and stand no nonsense from them. Myself and my two cobbers, now known to the sergeants as 'The Three Musketeers' and to the sergeant-major as 'The Three Bloody Dagoes' – we had all three grown black, turned-up moustaches and were all three very much alike – were chosen as members of the guard, and we had a comfortable time of it crossing the Arabian Sea and running up the Red Sea.

The guarding of the prisoners had its humorous aspects, for we took an immediate liking to the German lads, pronouncing them fine fellows who had but done what they had conceived to be their duty, however unpleasant that duty had been from our point of view. Indeed we became vastly friendly with them, hopefully exchanging addresses with them and inviting them out to Queensland at the end of the war, while they gave us just as warm invitations to go to Germany to their homes. I don't know whether any of them got as far as Queensland, but I certainly never got round to going to Hamburg to spend a holiday with the parents of a very charming youth who had given me a most cordial invitation thither.

The poor devils had evidently been caught with their pants down, so to speak, for they had come aboard the *Omrah* in rags and tatters of all kinds. As we came into Suez, our officers had a whip-round for them, and each man was presented with a pair of trousers and a singlet. The morning we transferred them to the ill-fated *Hampshire* the full guard was drawn up on deck in two long files, between which the prisoners were to march to the gangway. But alas for this semblance of iron discipline over a conquered foe, as soon as the first prisoner stepped on deck he offered his hand to the nearest member of the guard, and the transfer was accomplished amid general handshaking. Next day as we steamed into the Canal, the prisoners assembled on the fo'c's'le head of the *Hampshire* and cheered us roundly.

It was while we were coming up the Red Sea that we learned what was to be our destination: Egypt to finish our training. On a bitterly cold December morning we drew in to Alexandria. As usual, 'No leave' was the cry of the authorities, but that did not prevent many of the Australians taking it anyway this time, some of them going ashore in the bumboats that swarmed round the ship as she anchored, while others swam ashore when the bumboats had had a few shots fired into them by the guards if orders to them not to approach within a certain distance were not observed.

For another forty-eight hours we were held on the anchored ship, and every one of these hours seemed to us like a year. We were disembarked on Monday 6th December, I think, were shot into trains and by 11 p.m. that night were lying in the sand somewhere outside Cairo. In a thick, clammy mist we had our iron rations or part of them for supper, composed ourselves to rest as best we could and arose shivering next morning to finish the unpalatable rations off for our breakfast. The upper air was clearing a bit as we ate, and two huge triangular-looking masses of masonry, the tops of the pyramids, stood out dimly above the mist. A pal of mine, Ned Kelly, was still lying wrapped in his overcoat on the sand, making pretence to be asleep. 'Wake up, Ned,' I adjured him. 'Forty centuries of history are looking down at you.' 'F——- you and your history,' retorted Ned. 'I'd rather my b——y breakfast was looking up at me.'

Much of the Australian reputation for indiscipline and wild conduct was acquired during the time of our training in Egypt. We were coming under British administration for the first time, and there was much about it that we did not like. We set about amending it in our own way. For instance, we did not at all cotton on to the idea of sleeping on the sand in our overcoats while the ordnance stores were full of blankets and groundsheets, which could not be issued to us because there was some difficulty connected with signatures for vouchers. We just raided the stores and took the blankets and groundsheets and to hell with the vouchers. No camp kitchens had been set up, and for days we had to make do with black tea and very tasteless army bread. My section went on strike about this. When told to quick march the dust-brown ranks stood fast. The whole section was being marched to the guard room when Jock Roberts came on the scene. 'Fall out, boys,' said Jock. 'Gather round me and just listen to me.'

In five minutes the little bandy Geordie had us in tears over our striking and in another five we were marching behind him singing. But ever afterwards when for any reason the food was not all it should have been, we just went on strike. As the men had it, they knew as much about hunger and could stand as much of it as anyone else, but that food should go wrong in a training camp was a sign that somebody was not doing his job or was blundering. Then there was the attempt to set up an officer caste by proclaiming that none but officers could go into certain hotels in Cairo. Cairo was then full of Kitchener's dugout brass hats, who wanted these hotels reserved for themselves and their rather scraggy womenfolk. The Australians just went into these *sancta sanctorum*, and hotel dragomans or MPs seeking to prevent their doing so were thrown out into the street. The Australian would not subscribe to the theory that what the soldier saluted was not the man, but the uniform. He refused to salute the uniform unless he respected the man inside it. What probably riled them most was the arrangements made for the sale of beer to them. This was done under some relic of army administration in the days of Queen Elizabeth I, if not of the days of Alfred and his Saxon fyrd. A firm of civilian contractors to the army had the monopoly of the sale of beer to the troops. It was of very poor quality, and the price of it in the firm's big marquees was much higher, the Australians found out, than that charged in the pubs in Cairo. About the same time they came across a report in an English paper that the firm was declaring a forty per cent dividend. The 3rd Brigade seemed to have more about which to grumble in regard to this firm of contractors than did the 1st New South Wales troops or the 2nd Brigade (troops from Victoria). At any rate, they were more vocal about their wrongs. One night they brought matters to a head by burning down the marquee.

These and similar misdeeds got reported back to Australia and to London. Oily politicians came and lectured us. 'All bull,' said the Australians. I don't know what wrought grace within the 1st and 2nd Brigades, but what worked it within the 3rd was an address from our brigadier-general, a spare Lancastrian. He told us bluntly that we were making damned fools of ourselves, disgracing our country and causing its name to stink in the nostrils of the whole world. We reckoned it was time to draw in a bit. We would have our fun in a milder way, but we would make ourselves the finest soldiers in the world.

We trained until, as the Irish say, we were jumping out of our skins. After about two months of this rigorous training the brass hats began to come along to inspect us on our 'battalion' days, 'brigade' days and on our occasional 'divisional' days. It seemed to us Queenslanders that we often came in for compliments from these military gods, and that we were not just puffing ourselves up was shown one night towards the end of February, 1915, when the colonel, preceded by a bugler, entered our mess hut. The bugler blew a mighty blast, and he probably had need to do just that to get silence. 'Men,' said the colonel, and for once his usually squeaky schoolmasterly voice had resonance, 'I'm proud to tell you that the 3rd Brigade has been passed fit for active service and prouder still to tell you that the 9th Battalion has been adjudged to be the fittest and best trained battalion of that brigade.'

'Tarantara, could you keep one down?' we roared as we leaped across tables and forms and shook hands with one another. But active service was not yet just around the corner.

13

The next halting place in the wanderings of the ATA (the Australian Touring Army), as we now called ourselves, was as antithetical as well could be to a desert camp in the vicinity of a great city. On a blusteringly cold March dawn we found ourselves gazing at the foam-created wavelets of a land-locked bay, entrance to which, if one were to judge from the seemingly complete circle of hills around it, could only have been secured by our transports leaping over them. As the rattling, vermin-ridden old Canadian cattle boat on to which another battalion of the 3rd Brigade bad been packed with us Queenslanders at Alexandria could not be imagined doing anything so sprightly as leaping, we inferred that she must have crept into this bay by some winding passage invisible to us from our position inside it.

Where we were we had not the least idea until told we were near a village called Mudros on the Greek island of Lemnos, which was somewhere in the eastern Mediterranean and close to the coasts of Asia and what was now left of Turkey in Europe. In that spring of 1915 the Australians almost admitted that Mudros Harbour was as beautiful as was Sydney Harbour. Up from the water's edge spread a plain of green fields backed by slopes of cultivation merging into a background of miniature mountains. Tucked in between sea and hills were brown-roofed villages, around which clustered windmills that looked like giant short-tailed birds standing on their heads.

Entirely ignorant of whither we were proceeding, we had left Alexandria four mornings before. At first we thought we were bound for France, but our boat steered not towards the setting sun. Dawn on the following morn came not to us from astern but from starboard, and that day and the next the boat was grunting its way among islands that came endlessly into and receded from view, all bleak and barren as seen by the naked eye, but, seen through glasses, dotted with picturesquely situated little towns and ribbed with valleys of the most delicate green. From what geography we could muster we reasoned that we were steaming through the Cyclades, and even Byron got quoted at least to the extent of:

'The Isles of Greece; the Isles of Greece.'

Our destination might be, we argued, Salonica, Smyrna, Alexandretta. But why the devil this place, Lemnos?

However, in it the Queenslanders were given something about which they might again spread their tail feathers. They were the first Allied troops to land on Lemnos. On Saturday afternoon, March 7th, I think it was, the battalion was ordered into life-boats. We were assured they were just that, but they must then have been in the water for the first time in many years. They leaked like sieves, and while we were being towed across the harbour in them, we baled like demons with our mess tins. We got safely to a little rickety wooden quay with plenteous gaps in its flooring and, making ourselves, if pride could add to our stature, giants, with chests expanded and heads held high, we marched up the winding, earthy lane that served Mudros for a high street. At the doors stood wrinkled crones, beefy-looking matrons, ox-eyed maids, all with eyes wide and all muttering something that sounded like 'Pollee! Pollee!' This I took to be a variation of our old friend of earlier days, the classical 'polu' or 'polloi' though I could not settle to my satisfaction whether the women meant 'many' or 'big' by the exclamation. To my cobbers, of course, I gave the latter translation as the one more flattering to us. So, we tried to stick out our chests still more and to the piercing strains of our bugle band we hummed, not without thought of the desire-exciting maids in the doorways,

What's the matter with father?
  He's all right.
  He's put the cook in the family way.
  He's seven and six a week to pay.
What's the matter with father?
  He's all right.

We swung round another lane to a green hill over the harbour, learning for our comfort these things: tents would be brought ashore some time; when, no guess could be made. Meanwhile we'd have to do with groundsheets and blankets in the open air. For some time, duration again unknown, we'd have to make do with half rations of bully beef and bread. Pay would come when it would arrive if ever. All Greek villages were out of bounds. Any interference with the island women would be regarded as rape and as such would by Australian law be punishable by death. To us Queenslanders, as the best trained and best disciplined battalion of the division, had been given the honour of being put ashore to prepare a base camp for a whole army. We must show ourselves worthy of such an honour. So flattered, we would have endured much worse, and anything looked better than remaining cooped up in that filthy old scow which had brought us from Alexandria with its holds scarcely head high and its runneled floors stinking of bovine urine. So, on a not very warm night we spread our groundsheets and blankets on the weed-grown furrows between the mounds left by badly dug potato drills. Very cheerfully we spent the Sunday carting water from a village pump that no more than trickled it out to our most valiant pumping efforts, while two of us who had once known a lot of classical Greek tried to hold conversation with some very smartly turned out Greek sailors anxious to start their English studies by learning the meanings of words vulgarly used with regard to sex matters. We had drawn one pound a man before leaving the boat and with as much of that sum as had escaped the clutches of the crown and anchor (gambling dice) kings we bought food, manna-like loaves, long and white, plates of rice pudding and even occasionally bottles of wine from the Greek pedlars.

Surprisingly enough the tents were brought ashore to us in a couple of days, but not until we had had a thorough soaking one night as we lay out on the hillside while a thunderstorm raged over the eastern Mediterranean. With the eagerness of homeless people moving into a prefab we pitched those tents, and cut furrows around them in case we had to endure other deluges.

The night we got the tents up was the first of many very happy nights on Lemnos, nights that I would dearly like to live over again. And our days were happy too. We did very little military training, just an occasional field day, when we met the other battalions of the 3rd Brigade, who professed great envy of us that we were ashore while they, 'sick, sore, lame and lousey', as they said, were still cooped up in their transports in the harbour. Most of our time, if the weather permitted of our being about at all, was spent on fatigue work. We navvied while our engineers laid on a water supply from small streams in the hills. We quarried and carried down to the harbour stones for a new quay they were building. We carried stores up from the old quay, great boxes and bales of all sorts of foodstuffs and hospital gear, even bales of forage for a couple of thousand horses that must have been laughing their heads off at us and were being taken from their lines a couple of times a day for exercise by squat little Englishmen. We were often hungry. It occurred to us to query why the animals couldn't be used to cart the food to us instead of our having to hump up food for them. No doubt, there was some deep military reason for this reversal of the usual roles of man and horse.

And soon we came to an arrangement with Jock Roberts by which we of his platoon volunteered quite gladly for fatigue work at any hour of the day or night. As the army was not feeding us properly, we decided that, as far as possible, we'd look after our own comforts at the expense of the army. When in shifting stuff we came across anything in the way of food or anything else likely to be of use to us, we, careful of the eleventh commandment (thou shalt not get caught), appropriated it. Thus we acquired many things that went far towards making our tent seem homely. We had several buckets, a couple of axes, for which QM blokes spent days in vain search, a brazier, for which the cook lines unwittingly supplied wood. We had soap, plenty of it, candles, rolls of toilet paper and several quarter-pound tins of Virginian tobacco, which was purloined from between the feet of a British quartermaster who had taken his stand over them with an oath that no gore-bespattered Australian need think himself clever enough to steal anything from him. He thought he knew all their tricks. He didn't. For days we had liver and bacon, the former acquired from a field slaughter-house to which some of us had been sent on fatigue, the bacon abstracted from an immense QM store which we had been stocking up. Our best score in this game of appropriation or misappropriation was registered one night when we were summoned to the quay for an urgent job of store shifting. In a chaos of stuff to be lugged up the hill we came on a case marked 'Cognac'. We consulted Jock Roberts about it, and we soon had the case wrapped in blankets and stowed away in his tent. The case contained the very best cognac in bottles of pocket size. While the cognac lasted, Mr Roberts would stroll of an evening along the tents of his platoon, slip a bottle from his overcoat pocket into each of the four tents, returning to ours, in which he would sit for a few minutes smoking his long-stemmed pipe. There was just enough of the cognac in a bottle to give a taste to the tea we brewed. Jock would speculate on the future that was in store for us and himself. Poor little man! He was very despondent about his own. He felt that the Turks had a bullet with his number on it and that they would discharge it pretty quickly in the scrap that was looming between us and them. He could not bring himself to think that he would never again see Queensland, his wife or his children. He proved quite right in his doleful presentiment. He was killed quite early on the morning of the Australian landing on Gallipoli.

We welcomed rainy days, of which there were many, because on such days we had no 'spasms'. We pined not when sleety clouds blanketed the hills on the farther side of the harbour and the increasingly more numerous outlines of transports and war vessels could be seen but dimly through the mists that lowered over the restless waters. In the forenoon we would get the brazier going, and the sixteen of us would sit around while the liver and bacon was being fried and the tea brewed 'billy' fashion. In our very small tin dish the liver and bacon could be cooked only for one man at a time, and when the sixteenth man was having his whack of it the first would be expectant of a second helping.

At 9 p.m. each night the 'billy' would be set going, and soon we'd be blowing the wraiths of steam that would curl up from the dark, sweet fluid in our mess tins and munching the sweet Greek bread plentifully spread with jam. As a result of our being set on guard one night over a QMs tent we had an ample supply of tea, sugar and buckets of jam. An hour or so later after jest and story we'd settle down to sleep. Around our tent pole we had constructed a rack for our rifles: to the top of it we had nailed bars on which to hang our web equipment. Even with this economising of space it took some adjustment to get the lot of us fully stretched out. Snorers were placed near the tent door so that they could be kicked out without much trouble.

Of course, into this existence on Lemnos which we had made so idyllic there would creep discontent. A lot of it was due to the contrast between the freedom permitted to a division of French troops who were in camp quite near us and the restrictions under which we suffered. The French could stroll through the village, visit its bars, ramble at will through our lines while it was a court martial for us if we as much dared set foot in Mudros or in the French camp. More of the discontent was over pay. Indeed money was so scarce amongst us that the gambling schools had ceased to operate. Their kings and frequenters were by this time reduced to playing solo whist for the fun of the thing. In the evenings especially we would indulge in mutterings. The money was due to us. Why the hell couldn't it be paid? We wouldn't soldier for them any longer. We would join the French, who always seemed to have money to spend and with whom a man was treated as a man. The easy relations of the French with their officers had made a great impression on us. We would even join the British. Tommies got but a bob a day, but the point was they got it, or we thought they did. Once while this assertion of desperate intent was in full blast, I lay trying to read my way through a copy of the *Anabasis*, which a villager had given me. I happened to come on the passage in which the Greeks told Cyrus, 'No more pay, no more soldiering.' I sniggered. The others demanded to be told the reason for my laughter. Prolonged was their mirth when I translated the passage for them. Saying the soldier hadn't changed much in over two thousand years, they would have the whole story of Xenophon and his ten thousand men. So, I delivered myself of the first of my many lectures on Xenophon's tale of heroism.

At first we had deluded ourselves that the reason for our being at Lemnos was that when the British and French fleets had knocked the Gallipoli forts to hell we would be required for mopping up and garrison duties on the Peninsula. The odds that the Australian Touring Army would keep on touring shortened considerably when in the middle of March the fleets got a thorough doing in an attack on these forts. We began to see that there was a strong likelihood of something much more serious than mere garrison duties ahead of us. We became brighter, finding in the prospect of real fighting a new manhood or a new childishness. At the same time spring was making its coming to the island more forcefully felt every day. The weather was warming up; the grass had a greener sheen; the wheat was peeping above the rude cultivation of the islanders; the vines were wreathing the walls of the houses in green draperies. It seemed too fair a scene to leave for a rendezvous with death.

Some time about the end of March we got word that the commander-in-chief of the entire expedition for an attack on the

Peninsula would be Sir Ian Hamilton, a dugout in excelsis. But our sergeant, now a Scot named Findlay holding a DCM, had soldiered somewhere with the old buffer and vouched for his being all right. He was coming ashore to inspect the Queenslanders, and we were to be on our best behaviour for that inspection. Hamilton has described that inspection from his own angle in his *Gallipoli Diary*. It took place on a bitterly cold morning, and he was an hour late coming along for his inspecting. We had to stand under arms waiting for it while an icy wind blowing from the snow-capped mountains of Asia Minor cut through us to the marrow. Hamilton had recorded of us that we were magnificent cannon-fodder. At the end of his inspection, during which, I remember, I came under his displeasure because there was something wrong with a button on my tunic, our colonel asked him if he would like to see us at some field work. Hamilton resignedly said he would. We were taken down to the sea and told that the ridge on which stood two of the island's windmills was an enemy position, which we were to capture at the point of the bayonet. Hamilton has an unflattering reference to us as being like so many Don Quixotes tilting at windmills. What he did not spot was that three or four of the islanders' nice fat sheep were busily grazing on a sort of saddle of ground between these windmills. The notion came to us that like the swagman in 'Waltzing Matilda' we'd stow these jumbucks in our tucker bags and have them for dinner as an agreeable change from the stringy buffalo meat on which we were then being fed. We were charging the sheep, not the windmills. With a thousand yelling Australians behind them with fixed bayonets these sheep must have had about the biggest fright sheep ever had. How they fled to other pasture.

Early in April we were ordered onto a transport. This was another Canadian cattle boat, smaller and, if that were possible, even filthier than the one on which we had been shifted from Alexandria to Mudros. Besides the 9th Battalion there were dumped on to her swarms of brigade engineers and medical details. She was horribly overcrowded. Men would wander round her at night looking for a few inches of space in which to lay their blankets down for sleep.

There appeared to be an utterly inadequate supply of rations aboard. At any rate, we were put back on half issue and that was nearly always just bully beef and bread, with milkless and sugarless tea. 'Skinny' Heaton, seasoned old warrior of many of Britain's frontier wars, could nearly always find a way out of food or other difficulties. He had constituted himself our company cook, but even his versatility could not make an appetising meal out of bully and bread. He had for his period as a civilian been a stage hand with a Shakespearean touring company. He went about declaiming, 'A spud! A spud! My kingdom for a spud!' Skinny's escapades with the Australians would require a book for themselves alone.

In addition to the shortage of food we had a plenitude of vermin. By this time we were just crawling with them. We tried washing our clothes in the sea, diving into the harbour and washing them as we swam about, but the damned 'cooties' appeared to thrive on salt water.

One good thing resulting from our return to the transport was that we got some of our arrears of pay. We were daily being drilled in getting into small boats and being taken ashore in them. When ashore we could buy from the Greek pedlars. We'd return to the ships with their long loaves strapped to our packs and hunks of their cheese in our haversacks. Sometimes if they and we were quick about it, we could get drink from them: a potent spirit that was, largely, I suspect, methylated spirit, but in bottles and with labels on them as clean as if they had just been placed on the shelf in a spirit store. '————'s best brandy', said the labels.

These landing practices were tricky affairs. It was no small feat to climb down the ship's side by a rope ladder while one had one's full equipment on one's back and then drop from the ladder into a cockle-shell bobbing up and down on the water. I suppose we improved with practice; at any rate, we came to do it fairly quickly and with indrawn breaths instead of lurid oaths as we barked our knuckles against the discoloured plates of the ship. We had several experiments at landing by night.

All this was giving us to infer that the day was coming closer when we would be called upon to prove ourselves in some deadly enterprise. Our speculations as to the time and place of this proving were set at rest by our being told on April 15th of the time and place. Fifteen hundred men of the 3rd Brigade, five hundred from each of the 9th, 10th and 11th Battalions, i.e. Queenslanders, South Australians and West Australians, would steal ashore just before dawn on Sunday morning, April 25th, at a selected spot on the Gallipoli Peninsula. If all went well, they would surprise and get possession of a Turkish fort called Gaba Tepe. If things did not go so well, and it was quite possible they would not, we were to seize a beachhead large enough to allow room for the disembarkation of the rest of the Australian and New Zealand divisions. In orders and in lectures there was explained to us the nature of the terrain on which we would have to fight, and it was emphasised to us that if we once got ashore we must die to the last man rather than retreat. Surrender must not be thought of: the Turks would maltreat us, and we were given very unpleasant details as to what that maltreatment would be. We must husband ammunition. The bayonet was to be our only weapon. We must expect to endure both hunger and thirst. There was no telling when any supplies of food could be got ashore to us, and the Turks would be sure to have poisoned any sources of water we might come across.

To all this we responded by the unprintable equivalent of *Caesar! morituri te salutant.* A and B Companies of the 9th were to be the Queenslanders' contribution to the fifteen hundred thus flung forward to almost certain death and we were to be the guiding party, the right of the line in this almost superhuman endeavour.

Had we foreseen the events of that Sunday morning, being the right of the line was an honour we could have done without. It was upon us that the brunt of Mustaf Kemal's counter-attack fell, and it rather made mincemeat of us.

14

About noon on Saturday, April 24th, 1915, a destroyer drew up to our transport, took the five hundred of us Queenslanders aboard and hared off with us across Mudros Harbour to an old battleship named *The Queen.* The men of that battleship, by having a hot meal waiting for us, earned our deep gratitude to the British Navy. It was the first square meal we had had for over a month, and we ate till the skins of our stomachs threatened to split. Later on that afternoon they gave us a fine filling tea. Throughout the evening they would pile tinned stuff of all kinds on us, though with the seventy pounds of equipment and ammunition with which we were already loaded most of us had as much as we could carry.

Late in the afternoon, four battleships, *The Queen* leading, headed out into the Aegean Sea. I have, of course, since read descriptions of us as kingly beings going forth to a pageant of death. As to us such writing was just plain rot. Most of us, though aware that we were on no picnic, headed for the gambling schools with the few shillings we had managed to keep thus far. 'Pretty sure to get killed,' called out the gambling kings. 'What good will your money be to you then? Better have a run for it before that happens.' Some of these kings had as much as five hundred pounds on them when we landed.

A little after midnight *The Queen* stopped dead. We got orders to put on our equipment and assemble in absolute silence on her main deck. And in absolute darkness too. The striking of a match or the least indulgence in our customary shouting would be fatal to our enterprise. Who contravened in either respect would be shot out of hand, a punishment that, I thought, would defeat its own end. No threat was necessary to bring home to us the necessity for absolute silence. No voice was raised above the merest whisper.

Cobber shuffled silently to cobber, shook hands and very softly muttered their goodbyes. Then we moved along to the side and crawled down the swaying ladders to the small boats screened from the light of the moon by the shadow of the battleship. Into these small boats we settled as best we could, and the best was damned uncomfortable. We waited, of course. One asked one's self why that waiting could not have been done in comfort on the big ship, but one forbore to curse this last sample of army 'frigging about'. The boats rocked to a gentle swell. The waves danced in lines of light along the sea.

I guessed that our waiting was for the setting of the moon. Never, if time be measured in heartbeats, did the moon make slower setting. And as it set, for the battleship swaying with the currents could not always keep us hidden, it sank into the sea as a great disc of angry red, a colour which I and, no doubt, many of the others interpreted as an evil omen of the hours to come. With its setting it was as if a great lamp were switched off, the world was palled in darkness.

It may have been about 3 a.m. when the boats began to move. From ahead there came faintly to our ears the chugging of a launch; from beside us the ripple of water against the sides of our small boat. We could distinguish other white specks on the water in snake-like coils. These specks straightened out into a line.

In the succeeding days war correspondents vied with one another in finding words to describe the epic gallantry of that Australian landing. The greatest thing about it and about us was, I think, that without sending up shrieks to Heaven we endured those agonising hours of waiting by the battleship and that maddeningly slow passage to land. Few breaths can have been drawn without constraint, but the uttered word I never heard. The Australians were out to prove they could be as quiet as the next blighters.

We may have been about half the distance from the battleship to land when a light – or was it a star? – blinked ahead of us. But a star never twinkled so methodically as this one was blinking. The enemy was signalling. There was to be no surprising them. Our adventure was now to be on the 'not so well' note; get ashore somehow, grip a bit of Turkish soil and die, if needs be, probably die in the holding of it.

In minutes that each seemed a lifetime, a cloud – or was it land? – loomed up ahead of us. It was land, for it took on contours and at the foot of it there was a strip of white. It won't be long now. 'Jesu, Maria! I am nigh to death.'

A few yards more and the boat slowed down. The navy launch was cutting adrift from us. In each boat were eight heavyweight Australians who had had special training in the use of these outsize oars known as sweeps, which they had up till now been holding erect. There was whispered command of, 'Down oars, boys!' As the boat gathered speed again under their impulse, there was a sound as of a stone striking the water about a yard to the right of us. There was a dull explosive sound from the cliff tops, then two more splashes in the water yards behind us; two dull explosions from the cliffs, then a drum roll of noise, into which cut a sharper, angrier hissing of things over our heads. We were under rifle and machine-gun fire. For some seconds panic hovered near us.

Instead of yielding to it we laughed loudly. 'Steady, lads. Keep your bloody heads,' had shouted a boy of sixteen. 'The bastards couldn't hit a haystack.' His name deserves recall for record in the annals of warfare. It was Hillier. He had a nickname, of course – what Australian didn't? – but I don't remember what it was. He and his brother aged seventeen were in the other section of Mr Roberts's platoon.

To our great good fortune the Turks continued to fire high. Even a laugh might not have held us together if there had been a half-dozen of squirming, dying bodies in that boat. It again stopped dead. There came a shout – I don't know from whom – of 'Jump for it, lads!' We, who the night before had been made

123

to walk through boiling fat so that we should not get our feet wet in landing, just hurled ourselves into the sea. I came up the five foot eleven of me with the salt water lapping about my neck. Each early step I tried I went under, but there was nothing for it save struggle on. I struggled, and the water was receding down my chest, my stomach; it was soon up only to my hips, then only to my knees, and I could run in a shackled sort of way. That strip of beach was the world to win.

At last I reached it and fell over other prostrate forms. Had half a million Turks with gleaming bayonets been there, we could not have done otherwise than lie there till the water drained out of our clothes, till we had coughed out what of it we had swallowed. When we were just only plain wet and had got back a little of our breath, we rose and made a short dash to the foot of a little cliff by which the hillside made a sudden plunge to the beach. There we lay, slipping off our packs and wondering what the devil was to come next.

For us it came very informally. Jock Roberts stood up, shook himself and looked round at us.

'What about it, boys? Shall we have a go at them?'

'What the hell do you think we came here for, Mr Roberts?' summed up the answers.

Charging for a less precipitous point on our right, our platoon went tearing up the hill to the battle-cry of 'Eggs a cook, you bloody bastards! Musquels. Imshi. Up to ———. You ——— pigs. Ibn kelp.' The hill rang with bellows of scurrility and blasphemy that drowned the chatter of rifle and machine-gun fire. After our wracking silence we could now yell our fill. And how we yelled as, like greyhounds, we bounded up these almost precipitous hillsides!

Here and there a man was killed or wounded, but we had been very sternly reminded that our role was not cast for works of mercy. The dead were dead, and the wounded were to be left wherever they had fallen until such time as found by the stretcher bearers.

When we got to the top of the first ridge, we came on some abandoned shallow trenches. Nowhere was there a Turk in sight, but rumours spread among us of there having been sharp fighting to the left of us, of fellows we knew having been killed, of Queenslanders capturing Turkish guns, of one Tipperary giant named Bill Byrne having leapt into a trench, bayoneted four of the Turks and slung them out over his shoulder as if they had been sheaves of wheat. I met Bill afterwards in hospital in Egypt. He had not a word to say about this exploit attributed to him, but then if it had been mentioned in his hearing Bill would have asked, very probably, what the hell else was he to do with the bastards.

Of a surety whatever Turks had held that first ridge had been routed, and we may be pardoned for thinking that the way to Constantinople lay open before us.

Perhaps in these moments it did. On my table when fifteen or sixteen years ago I first drafted this chapter there lay newspaper cuttings which showed that twenty years afterwards experts were arguing that point. In my own unmilitary way I have always thought that the struggle for Gallipoli was lost for the first time between 5 a.m. and 8 a.m. that Sunday morning. Had an advance by these fifteen hundred Australians been fully supported in these three hours, they could have been right across the Peninsula.

As it was, we sat about for these three hours in a mood of exultation. Then came an order to move forward at a left incline. As though we were on a picnic we strolled rather than marched along these hilltops. The shrubs that covered them were in full leaf. Little flowers peeped out to greet the sun, which was turning the Aegean into a sheet of silver, darkly spotted by oncoming warships and transports. We were advancing by what appeared to be a roughly made grass-grown road, along which rippled a little stream, and so peaceful was everything about us that the crashes from Gaba Tepe and the duller booms from the British battleships might have been sound effects on a distant stage.

Desultory rifle fire broke out ahead, and the picnic feeling ended. Orders were shouted at us, but in these orders and the interpretation of them there was much confusion. Some were for going forward, some were for holding back, some were for seeking cover, not that there was much of that available on our exposed ridge. Our platoon had come to a knob of ground that sloped down to a narrow valley, on the opposite edge of which was a line of scrubby trees. Jock Roberts halted us on that knoll and told us to dig with our entrenching tools head shelters for ourselves. 'Something tells me,' he said, 'that this is the beginning of a counter-attack. We'd better be ready to meet it.'

We were frantically plying the entrenching tools when word came to us from the left that we were to resume our advance at the double. Others of the Queenslanders were charging madly for the ridge. 'It's murder,' commented Jock, 'but we'd better obey.' They were his last words. A few seconds later he was dead.

None of us reached the shrubs. The dreamy quiet of half an hour before was transmuted into pandemonium. Aeroplanes, whether Turkish or British, we could not say, droned above us; Turkish guns roared earsplittingly from somewhere in front; warships boomed from the sea behind us, their shells whining over us; the crackle of rifle and machine-gun was like the rattle of hail on a zinc roof. Australians were toppling over like ninepins. Birds, startled from the shrubs, were falling to earth as they started off on their curving flight.

What had happened is now well-known. Mustaf Kemal had hurried up a Turkish division with the object of driving us back into the sea. Every advantage was with the Turks. They were under cover: we were in the open; they had machine-guns and artillery: we hadn't even rifles, for in our scramble to get ashore the salt water and sand had rendered them useless. We had only bayonets and could see nothing on which to use them. Our machine-gunners were trying desperately to set up their two guns while they turned their heads aside as from a storm; they were being picked off like partridges. Their young officer was the very first to fall. Mounted, the guns spluttered feebly, choking after a few rounds.

We had no intention of letting a mob of Turkish bastards drive us into the sea, but we sought every inch of ground that could afford us shelter from this inferno. In this search we became much disorganised, and the loss of comradeship or cobberdom was very demoralising. And we suddenly became aware that we were very tired. We waited in hopeful desperation for a Turkish charge. According to the book of words as it had been explained to us the Turks should have made that charge. But they did not. They just kept on with that infernal crack-crack of theirs from shelter. When things were at their worst with us, a Victorian battalion, which had landed dry-shod, came cavorting uproariously over the ridge behind us and carried us forward some distance with it. But not quite to that belt of shrub. Strong language was no longer producing much effect on the stolid Turks.

So confused had everything become round about ten o'clock that we had no longer the least semblance of formation. To judge by the whines of bullets possibilities of death presented themselves from all angles. Not an officer was to be seen. They had, I take it, been picked off by sharpshooters. NCOs were rare. We wandered about seeking formations to which to attach ourselves.

I should judge it to have been about midday when a little group of us Queenslanders, unable to get in touch with the 9th Battalion, joined in with a company of Victorians holding a grassy knoll on our extreme right. They told us they had been posted at that spot to prevent a Turkish flanking movement against the Australian beaches. They gave us cigarettes – our own cigarettes and tobacco had gone into mush seven hours before – lauded us as heroes of the landing party and advised us, as we must be worn out, to have a 'camp', i.e. a rest. We lay down on the grass, and the thunders from a battleship, a few hundred yards away, did not prevent us from falling into a very sound sleep.

We had some officers when I fell asleep. We had none when I woke up some time in the mid afternoon. Probably they had been sniped, for the fellow next to me was as dead as mutton, having been shot through the forehead. Nor, as far as I could see, had we any NCOs except a corporal. An informal council of war was being held. A rumour had come along that the whole Australian and New Zealand line, thought to be somewhere on our left, was advancing. Well, we'd advance too. The battleship could deal with any flanking movement by the Turks.

We advanced in all about three or four miles, the most pleasant advance made on Gallipoli. In some approach to order we rambled up and down slopes over country that might be described as 'park land'. Round hills far ahead of us, we could see men, dwarfed by the distance into little figures of fun, scampering towards some objective on our left. Their uniform was dark against the brown of the hills; so we judged they must be Turks. We sat down and watched them rather amusedly. In a valley between two of these hills a peasant was ploughing. Through dips in the hills behind us we could see a patch of the sea, on which a battleship was resting and very busily engaged in tossing shells into the ploughman's valley. It was just too bad that ploughman, oxen and plough disappeared in a cloud of hurtling earth.

I estimated the distance between us and the scampering figures to be two thousand yards. I had now acquired a serviceable rifle from a wounded Victorian, and, putting up the sights to that mark, I fired one shot. Insisting that I had fired without orders, the corporal and I had a heated argument as to whether or not he should have me shot.

After this argument we resumed our advance, but had not gone very much farther before doubt assailed us. This advance was far too easy, and though we had been keeping a good incline to the left, the line of the Australians and New Zealanders was nowhere in sight. We did not know that we had by this been newly christened 'Anzacs'. The place was oddly quiet. What crackle of rifle fire there was appeared to be behind us rather than in front. We held another council of war. A few hundred yards before us was a line of shrubs on the crest of a ridge. This ridge we would occupy and send out scouts to get the 'good oil' on the situation.

As we neared the crests we walked into hell. Rifles and machine-guns opened on us from the shrubs.

Men pitched to death in all sorts of bizarre attitudes. The chap on my left, a youth in his early twenties, a bright-faced lad who had been telling me of his interrupted studies at Melbourne University, stopped in the middle of a word, pitched forward and rolled over spasmodically, with his feet still twitching. There was a little circular hole in his forehead, a great irregular gash at the back of his head and a straggle of grey matter on the grass by the twitching feet. His brains had been blown out by an explosive bullet.

While I stood looking at him in wonder that life should so suddenly have ended for him, something struck me on the left side just about stomach level. Life would have ended for me then and my guts would have been sprinkled on the grass had it not been that this something had struck on two big reporter's notebooks which I had been using as a diary and which I carried in a poacher's pocket I had sewed inside the tunic from a purloined mailbag.

For a moment I thought that somebody had thrown a stone at me. I damned the thrower for trying on such a silly joke, then joined in the rush for the shrubs, but as I was within a yard of them, my left knee seemed to be wrenched away from the leg.

Murmuring, 'Carnally no more!', I went down like a log, breathing an ejaculatory prayer as I fell. I passed out.

When I came to, there was no khaki in sight save that on the dead. I dangled the left leg, finding much comfort in that the bone was not broken. But the knee was an awful sight. The breeches had been torn raggedly out of the puttee; great jagged edges of flesh were hanging down from and down to a wide gash extending from just beneath the kneecap to the rear of the joint.

What was I to do now? To make no bones about it, I decided I would run for it if I could. As I was trying with the totally inadequate field-dressing then issued to bind up the wound, an unscathed Queenslander crept up to me. He helped me undo the puttee, which we bound round the knee over the bandage.

We reckoned we were in a bit of a jam and that it was very

unlikely we'd either of us make the next water-hole. We thought we'd have a better chance of doing so if we tried separately than we'd have by keeping together. Gripping hands in a farewell that seemed very likely to be our last, we crawled off in different directions. It *was* our last, but he, too, got away safely for I heard of him afterwards as the crack sniper of the battalion. But I have never seen him since and I don't know what was his ultimate fate. Killed on the Somme, I think I heard.

Soon I came to a wadi with rough and stony sides. Recalling the 'Deadwood Dick' tales of my youth, I resolved to hide in it to nightfall and then steal back to the beach. Building a heap of stones for head protection, I lay drinking from my water bottle; it was the first drink I had had that day, and a most unpalatable beverage the cold tea proved.

A bullet scattered my heap of stones. Another whined along my back, cutting, I afterwards found, holes in both tunic and shirt and searing my spine. As I was apparently to be shot, better, I reflected, to be shot running than lying down. Breaking the rifle according to instructions given us for such emergencies, I slipped off all equipment, retaining but the water bottle. Some Turk, very likely rejoiced much over the finding of my haversack, which held two splendid hollow-ground razors, a present from a Brisbane cutlery firm to every Queenslander. It had all the little keepsakes and gifts from friends I cherished most; including a Latin version of Thomas à Kempis's 'The Imitation of Christ', bought for me in the author's home town by my German friend in South Africa, and a Latin version of 'Saint Augustine's Confessions'.

Run? How I ran! Never more heroically for cup or medal though in my South African days I had run myself to collapse for such trifles. Now, the prize was life itself, momentarily in peril. And life seemed such a precious small thing to keep, and it seemed to me there was such a lot of me, nearly six feet of me and thirteen stone, to let it slip from me. I ran on in the direction in which I judged to lie the little cove into which we had crept twelve hours ago. Hope grew with every unchecked stride. Bullets sang around me from all angles.

I had been running, I judge, over an hour when I saw on a hill far away on my right slouch-hatted men furiously wielding picks and shovels. They were digging the Anzac line which in our madness we had been seeking. I have no idea of where we had got to on that ill-conceived ramble of ours. I have since studied many sketch maps of that portion of Gallipoli, but just cannot make out where we had got to. Somewhere to the right of and behind that ill-fated Sari Bair Ridge, I think.

To reach the Australians would mean my going uphill, and I would be of little use to them if I did reach them. I thought I had better keep on going down the slope of the ground. Presently I came to a wider and much deeper wadi, in which there was a trickle of water. It would wind somewhere safe to sea. But its banks were very steep, almost straight down in fact. I made the descent into it by swinging out on and then dropping off the branch of a small tree overhanging it. The mud into which I sank nearly held me prisoner.

Presently I met other wounded hobbling along its bed. We exchanged the usual grim jokes of which the Australians are so fond in tight corners. A few yards from the mouth of the wadi we turned right along a stony track running along the shore and beneath vicious looking cliffs. This track brought us to a section of the beach over which fluttered Red Cross flags at the eastern end of the inlet now known as Anzac Cove.

There was death down here. Overhead there drifted small clouds from the almost continual bursting of shrapnel shells. There was a great fuss made in the British press just then about the Turks firing on the Red Cross. Right under these flags troops, supplies and munitions, even guns, were being brought to land. I expect the Turks made just as great a song and dance about the abuse of the Red Cross by the British.

Amid all the bustle of landing troops and supplies a few medical orderlies were struggling to attend to a crowd of wounded. One of them just spilled a bottle of iodine over my knee and put on a fresh bandage. There I was to lie for a couple of hours until they could find a boat to take us out to a ship. And while I lay, I got great comfort from one of the water carriers, Jack Deazley, one of the 'Three Musketeers', who came over to me with a four-gallon petrol tin of water in each hand, offered me one of them, telling me to drink as much as I liked but not to empty it, as, if I did, he would have to trot back and get it refilled. 'And there were a lot of snotty English bastards on the water launches.' I was to spare a cobber.

I didn't empty it, though I certainly lowered it by quite a few inches. It was a relief to have enough of something even if that something were only cold water.

Towards dusk I had the knee again soaked in iodine, had it rebandaged, had a card pinned on my shoulder and was dumped into a small boat that was to take about twenty of us out to a ship. The boat after some perilous episodes on its way out into the Aegean brought us alongside a transport, aboard which was the 14th Australian Battalion in feverish impatience to get ashore and join in the fun. The brave fellows cheered us wildly.

Three or four of us at a time, we were hoisted on deck by means of a cargo sling. Scrambling painfully to my feet from the frog-like heap in which this hoisting had deposited us, I was helped into a little hospital on the after deck, limped to a chair – with the cooling of the knee, I had the utmost difficulty in moving at all – flopped into a chair and, glad to be at rest at last, resigned myself to waiting for what I did not know. It would have to be preceded by waiting, anyhow.

An AAMC (Australian Army Medical Corps) chap came over to me and looked at the mess of bloody bandages round my knee. 'Hurt, does it, cobber?' he enquired. 'My oath! I bet it does. Can't do a damned thing for you tonight, anyhow. Something tomorrow if you're lucky. Say, how about a drink? Bet you could keep a long one down.'

I thought I could, a very long one. He came back to me with

a bottle of brandy in one hand and a beer tumbler in the other. He filled the tumbler nearly full and handed it to me.

'Get that down you, cobber. Good-night. See you at the next water-hole. If I were you, I'd have a shot at getting into one of those empty bunks.'

I sipped the brandy, every drop of it, and started on a crawl for an empty bunk. I must almost have made it, for orderlies found me asleep at nine next morning with my head on the edge of the bunk and my body and feet trailing on the floor. Well, I had had rather a busy day.

The orderlies woke me up and told me they were sorry the only breakfast they could give me was a hunk of dry bread and a mug of black tea. That was a lot more than at times in the past twenty-four hours I had dared to hope for.

15

While glad enough to have even dry bread and black tea and what looked like the probability of life (though the latter was not too assured as the German battlecruiser SMS *Goeben* was hurling high explosive across the Peninsula at all Allied shipping lying off the Gallipoli coast and some of this stuff had come uncomfortably close), I wondered at the lack of amenities on a ship equipped, as I had so far assumed, for the reception of wounded.

When my friend of the brandy bottle came along to me later in the morning all became clear. 'This isn't a Red Cross ship. She's nothing but a ruddy transport and a dirty old Chinese scow at that. The Red Cross boats were full up of wounded at two o'clock yesterday afternoon, and they have been pushing the poor devils on to this and other transports. They've been coming on to this tub all night. There's about nine hundred of you aboard now. One doctor and eight orderlies. He's the MO for the battalion that went ashore during the night, and we're his stretcher bearers. We're not orderlies really. No cooks. They've gone off to the fun up on these hills, and that's where we'd be, but the MO and we have orders to remain on here. Damned hard luck on us. God knows when the poor MO can get round to see you. Might manage it this evening, but you see there are hundreds much worse than you. He's been sawing off legs and arms all the night, and we've been chucking them in the sea just as if they were rotten spuds. God, man! If this was Sydney Harbour, we'd have all the sharks in the Pacific round this boat by this. We'll do what we can for you, but that'll be damned little. So long, cobber.'

That evening the doctor, white of face and looking very tired, reached me. 'H'm!' said he when to my intense agony the bandages, by this time stiff as leather, had been removed from the knee. 'You'll have to have that leg off. I haven't time to operate now. I'll stick a few stitches in it. They'll about hold it together till you get there.'

'Where's "there"?' I asked.

'Wherever the hell you're going,' he snapped back. 'How should I know? Mudros, Malta, Australia or England. You'll know when you get there.'

'There' turned out to be the Mena House Hotel at the foot of the little hill that leads up to the pyramids and the Sphinx. Medical boards waggled wise-looking heads over my leg there. Some were for having it off. Some were for leaving it on. All were agreed that on or off it would never be any good and that all question of my returning to the front was moonshine. They were, as it turned out, utterly wrong in their prophecies. I have never known a doctor right yet whether he was predicting well or ill of me. In a couple of days I was hobbling about; in a couple of years I was playing football for what passed for an AIF (Australian Imperial Forces) team. Indeed, though the wound was a bit slow in healing, the left leg became much the sounder of the two.

Hearing that the front was very definitely off, I wanted to be returned to Australia and was hoping that soon again I would be listening to Mr John's harmless thunderings and that Mary Gill would be pulling my leg or pinching my ear as she laid the plates of eggs and bacon or the plates of chicken and rice before me in the Tara Hotel. Unfortunately for these hopes the Australians were always querying what the men had been doing in civilian life. I don't know whether they were as clever as the British have been said to be at fitting square pegs in round holes, but the stout old colonel from Melbourne, who invariably acted as president of the medical boards, said that as I could write a little shorthand and do a bit of typing I would have to remain on in the army for clerical work. I foresaw that meant that I would very likely have to spend my time in fatigues or guard duties, for neither of which I had much liking. I demanded that he issue an order to camp commandants that I was to be employed for clerical work only and instead of having me court-martialled for insolence he gave me a letter to that effect. I was to show it to any Poo-Bah who attempted to put me on to other work.

I spent four months at Mena, four, on the whole, very delightful months, the first especially so. The night or two before landing on the Peninsula I had had some very good runs of luck at the crown and anchor dice boards; so I had a tidy sum of the 'ready'. The hospital was run on the extraordinary lines that one could go out and come in when one liked: there were no guards and no passes with which to contend, and, not irritated by regulations, against which they always fought tooth and nail, the Australians conducted themselves splendidly. I made many very fine friends. An Arab offered to hide me with his friends up the Nile and when the accursed war was over he would send me home to my mother. For, said he, when I was well, perhaps I would be sent off again to 'make battles', get killed and my poor mother would cry. When money was so short that we had to make do with ten charity fags a week, an Armenian gave me twenty cigarettes a day on condition that I would talk to him for an hour each day. A French couple, whose son, killed on the Western Front, bore, they said, a strange resemblance to me, wanted to get me out of the Australian Forces altogether, to adopt me and teach me the sugar manufacturing business. I got over the money stringency easily enough. Before leaving Australia I had alloted a portion of my pay to the Commonwealth Bank of Australia, and this sum I got transferred to me at Cairo. That was not the most advisable thing to do, but it got me out of the difficulty temporarily. And I have always been prone to temporary solutions of difficulties. Anyhow, I had a very pleasant July and part of August at Mena House.

About the middle of August, 1915, I was discharged from Cairo to a Base Details Camp. I there insisted on being paraded with my letter to the commandant. He put me on his staff as a shorthand typist. I saw he did not like a johnny thus, as it were, forced on him, and when in a couple of days there came a message that he should send into Headquarters, Cairo, a shorthand typist to replace a sergeant who was going out on service with the 2nd Australian Division, he bundled me in to the city.

There I was put to work in a section having to do with the supply of ordnance material to troops on active service. After a few really good arguments the Officer Commanding (OC) of this section and I became close friends. I concealed his delinquencies from prying higher authorities, and he gave me a lot of scope for my own.

Soon after I joined the Headquarters staff I had the good luck to win an Egyptian municipal lottery on a 2½d ticket. The sum was but eighty pounds, it is true, but that was wealth to me. It enabled me to rent a room in the flat of a delightful old French couple in Sharia Eloui. I had my meals in an Australian mess near the Moslem Al-Azhar University. I could spend my evenings in peace in my room, reading or writing. That autumn and winter of 1915 and the spring of 1916 I contributed quite a lot to English periodicals published in Cairo and got pretty well paid for these contributions.

Life was too sweet to last as I was enjoying it in 1916. I weekended always with my French friends at the sugar factory. Of a Saturday and Sunday evening we would sit out on their lawn on the banks of the Nile, sipping liqueurs, smoking the very best Egyptian cigarettes while we watched the huge feluccas laden with sugar cane swoop in to the landing ramps. Every Monday morning a steam launch took me across the river at Helouan, whence I caught a train that took me back to Cairo in ample time for me to be seated by my typewriter at 9 a.m. with the expression of a non-transgressor on my face. So long as I did my work when he wanted it done, the OC didn't care two twopenny damns what else I did. 'Mind you,' he warned me, when I explained to him once just how many regulations I was contravening habitually, 'I'm not telling you not to go on doing what you are doing. Still, go on doing it and just be careful.'

That I was careful is shown by the fact that although I broke every regulation, not once in five years did my name appear on a crime sheet.

However, 'the exigencies of the service', as I was learning to phrase it, were not likely to let me remain in Cairo just because I was having a very happy life there. Following the evacuation of Gallipoli the two Australian divisions were refitted at Tel el-Kebir and, supplemented by three new divisions made up of reinforcements who for some months had been kicking the desert sands about Cairo, were, in March, 1916, sent under their beloved 'Birdie' (later Field Marshal Lord Birdwood, but always 'Birdie' to the Australians) to France. (See letter in Appendix, pages 202–3.) It became clear that their Administrative Headquarters would have to shift to London or Paris, and in early May of that year the pen and ink warriors embarked at Alexandria for an unknown destination. I was by this time a staff-sergeant, a sufficiently exalted rank for a mere shorthand typist, and was officially transferred to the Australian Ordnance Corps.

On whatever day in 1916 England made its first experiment in summer time we came into Plymouth after a voyage not without incidents to be greeted by the sight of a green and pleasant land basking in a glorious sunshine after a night of rain. The sunshine was all the more welcomed by us as the voyage had been long and dismal. Through fear of submarines we had after we left Gibraltar been taken half-way across the Atlantic.

Bundled into a train that morning at Plymouth, we were shot that evening into a camp at Abbey Wood. The OC in charge of the troops for the removal was an elderly Australian millionaire, who had the idea that he could enforce discipline on his young countrymen. He had us locked into huts with very strict injunctions that we were on no account to break camp. We laughed at the injunctions, broke out of the huts, went to the nearest railway station, and spread ourselves in a sightseeing orgy over London, returning to camp that night or in many cases next morning to learn that we were all booked for orderly room. The Headquarters commandant, an Australian business expert, whose first military rank was that of major-general, thought that there was not much use in attempting to impose discipline on the Australians; he ordered the charge sheets against over five hundred of us to be torn up and had us marched into Westminster to get on with a job of work, that of taking possession of the Wesleyan Training College in Horseferry Road. There is a plaque outside the front gate of that institution recording that it was the Administrative Headquarters of the Australian Imperial Force from 1916 to 1919.

We had been afraid that we would be driven into barracks somewhere in London, and, therefore, learnt with no little relief that we would be paid 5/- a day subsistence allowance and allowed to live where we liked. We were given lists of boarding houses and allowed the rest of that day off to fix ourselves up with any landlady courageous enough to take on the task of lodging and feeding bunches of Australians. We were to be at work without any excuse at 9 a.m. on the Thursday.

And at work we were. I was in a new difficulty through our coming to London. Australian rates of wages were high compared with those then being paid in ordinary business circles, and Headquarters was soon swamped with girls who produced certificates to prove that they could write shorthand and hammer typewriter keys at about twice the rate I could manage. The order, therefore, went out that wherever possible male clerical labour was to be replaced by female equivalent. Luckily for me few of these girls could spell. Our OC was a man who required from the person taking dictation rather the interpretation than putting down symbols for his words. I could spell, and from long and close association with him I could read his mind. It might take me ten minutes to produce for his signature a letter that one of the little dears could turn out in five: but my letter could be signed right off, while theirs would have to be scrawled over with corrections and then sent back for retyping. So, I was kept on.

This particular OC was being shifted to a job in France and a man who had been Director of Ordnance Services for one of the Australian divisions there was coming to London to take his place. The newcomer had a frightful reputation for strictness. One evening the outgoing and incoming OC got into a huddle so that the newcomer could get the hang of things. It was one of the few hot evenings of that summer. I had come back to put in a spot of overtime in the polishing-off of some correspondence urgently required for dispatch next day. All doors and windows were open. I could hear every word of the confab between the major (newcomer) and the captain.

'Look here, Brinstead,' said the major, 'I didn't come here to work myself, but to see that other men work. I want a confidential man, who'll do all the work, give me an easy time; just have everything ready for my signature, not let any bugger bother me, be afraid of nobody from general to private, a glutton for work. Got anybody to fit that bill?'

'Well,' replied Captain Brinstead, 'There's a chap called Murphy. He works like a navvy, can swear like a bullocky, can remember any letter he's ever seen. I heard him telling General ——— the other day to get to hell out of it back to his unit. General ——— was demanding from us some article or other of equipment that was a field supply. The trouble is that he's the junior of all the permanent ordnance staff.'

'The man for my money!' exclaimed the major. 'I'll damned soon have him senior. Murphy's booked for promotion to warrant-officer Class I and ordnance conductor after I've given him a few days' trial. If he doesn't come up to scratch, I'll boot his backside out of it to Salisbury Plain or France.'

Dence, the then warrant-officer (WO) and ordnance conductor, was a youth of twenty, who neglected to obey a very early instruction given by the major about the removal of office gear to another part of the building to which we were being shifted. The removal was to be effected in our own time on Saturday afternoon so that work could restart promptly at 9 a.m. on the Monday.

'And nine a.m. does not mean nine-thirty,' warned the major.

At the indicated hour or a few minutes after it he stalked – stalk is the word for his movement; he was over six foot and over seventeen stone (a replica of Warwick Armstrong as Warwick was in 1921) – into his office. Just outside it in a little recess I was seated by my typewriter with my pointed pencil clipped by a little rubber band into my notebook. I had had very little to move on the Saturday, but Mr Dence had had a date to show a Hampstead lass around Richmond. He was, therefore, carting his many tables, chairs and ledgers to his new office. Glad of a break, three or four of his newly engaged female assistants were fluttering about. 'Send Mr Dence to me the moment he appears,' said the major.

'Mr Dence!' said he, when the WO came into him. 'I gave you an order on Saturday. I don't want to hear your reasons for not obeying that order. I can do without you. So can any bits of skirt you think more important than obedience. There's a very good train for Salisbury Plain at 4 p.m. See you catch it.'

'You're in charge here,' he said, coming out to me. 'You've got to see to everything here, mind you. I'm here to deal with very big questions only. The rest are your pigeon. Whatever you say I'll stand by you. You won't always be right, but I'll take the blame if there is any flying around. I'll never admit in the presence of a third-party that you've been wrong, but if you have, by heaven I'll give you the rough edge of my tongue when I get you by yourself. Satisfied?'

I agreed that that was as fair as fair could be.

That evening he came to me as he was going off.

'See here,' said he, 'at eight-thirty tomorrow morning there'll be a lorry with my kit on it in that yard down there. I want you to be there to meet it. Have my stuff shifted up here to my office. It'll mean half an hour earlier start for you. But I don't want my gear being bumped about London and getting lost. So, there must be no mistake about your being here to meet that lorry. If there is, I'll take you down there for three-minute rounds, and at the end of them you won't feel the least bit thankful to your mother for having brought you into this world.'

I looked at his massive chest and shoulders. Though I feared very much living up to the reputation he had been given of me, that of being afraid of nobody, I felt I must take the risk.

'All right,' said I. 'I'll meet your b——y lorry. But there's no need for you to be bringing my mother into it. Come down to the yard now and see how you feel about your own at the end of those three-minute rounds you're threatening me with.'

'Lad,' said he, putting out his hand, 'I like that sort of talk. Shake. I think we're going to be friends.'

Friends and, indeed, more than friends we became. Unluckily for me or luckily he was sent in a couple of months on a special mission to Australia. The man who took his place, an Australian, who, having joined up with the British Forces in London, had had some experience with the British Ordnance Services and was seconded back to the Australians, was often sick in hospital. From 1916 to the Armistice, therefore, the whole work of the supervision of the Australian Ordnance Services in Britain fell on me. I must not have discharged it too badly, for I got half a dozen Mentions in Despatches and was ultimately awarded a British Empire decoration. (See Base Records 7.4.20 in the Appendix, page 205.)

I was at the Armistice preparing to return to Australia under a scheme by which anybody who had joined the Australian Forces in 1914 was to have a six-month holiday in Australia. There'd have been no return from that holiday, I knew full well as I, on the morning of November 16th, 1918, filled in the application for it. The brass-hatted fellow who had come over from Australia the previous summer, to gain experience of ordnance work under war conditions, was not likely to oppose it. He and I had been squabbling like cat and dog and he was sure to give it his whole-hearted approval. Soon I would be running round Toowoomba again taking down the hems and the hash of Councillors Bigwind and Wildtalk.

I tossed the completed form aside, meaning later on to take it along to the Assistant Director of Ordnance Services (ADOS) and the commandant for their signature. Just then in walked the major, now a full colonel, as for past couple of years he had been Director of Ordnance Services to the Australian Corps in France.

'Murphy, old son, they have given me one hell of a big job. I'm to demobilise all equipment used by the Australians so far, return it to British stores and draw fresh equipment for six post-war Australian divisions. And do you know what I've told them? Well you can guess it was where they can they can stick the b———y job unless they grant me two conditions. One is that they send my wife and daughters over to London for a year, and the other is that I have you as my chief staff officer. They've agreed to both. So, how about it, old man?'

I showed him the application.

'Tear it up,' he bade me.

'What'll Wilson, Page and Tom Griffiths say to my going off like this with you?' I mentioned.

'Doesn't matter two howls from a dingo what these b———s say about it. They didn't treat you fairly. You should have been a captain ages ago. I'll have you made one as soon as I can get an establishment put through. Come along now. You know I've never let you down.'

I got up and went with him. The two of us toddled over to Victoria Street, where we put in practice his theory that we were not there to work ourselves but to see that others did the work we pointed out as needing to be done. So well had we organised things that soon we began to suffer from boredom. I got my brass tabs and my three stars all right, and I felt that the military hierarchy held no higher steps for me. The Australian government declared that it could not give passages out of Australia to the families of those other than permanent soldiers. The colonel then announced that if he could not have his family in London with him, he was going back to Australia to rear chickens and told the Australian authorities in London just where they could shove their demobilisation of stores. He selected a boat by which to return, selected his cabin on that boat and scooted off for home in July, 1919.

Neither all his efforts nor my urging was of any avail towards my getting permission to return to Australia on the same ship. Just because I could not go with him, I got my demobilisation in London, and one August morning after the colonel left I walked up Victoria Street, a civilian, though as yet in uniform. (See pages 204, 206 in the Appendix.) That morning the world, though the day was warm, seemed very cold and chill. A new world had been born, and I felt it would not be easy for me to fit myself into it. I was, as the Elizabethan has it, 'full feebly friended'. The representatives of London business houses, who a few months back would have licked my boots in the hope of getting an order for some purchase by the Australians, were at great pains to let me know now that my experience in handling or seeing to the handling of millions of pounds' worth of army stores made me especially unsuited for employment in any capacity as a civilian. I had by being demobilised in the UK entirely cut myself adrift from the Australians. As a matter of fact, just because I had not seen active service in France I had been ineligible for any of their many training schemes for refitting soldiers to earn a living as civilians. The world was chill, and I was often to find it so in the next ten years. Bold as I was, I could not think that my brief experience of journalism gave me any grounds for hope of employment on an English newspaper.

16

As the post-war slump was already in the offing by the autumn of 1919, jobs of any kind were very hard to come by. I could get one of a kind if I would invest in mushroom companies started by sharks eager to separate an ex-soldier from the few hundred pounds he had saved in the past five years. Even to such a simpleton as I it was obvious that investments in such companies was the equivalent of pouring money down a drain. What I did with mine was much the same as pouring it down a drain, but at least I had the satisfaction of spending it on myself. I spent it trying to bring to reality the dreams of writing that had so often cropped up in my unpractical mind. I bought a rickety old typewriter and betook myself to a delightful spot in the Chiltern Hills that would, I thought, furnish me with inspiration and provide excellent opportunity for study of rustic characters. I tried pretty hard, but I could not turn my inspiration or my rustic characters into a marketable product. In 1921, almost dead broke, I faced London once again.

There was positively nothing at all to be had by then except selling on commission. I became a 'knight of the road', one of twelve ex-officers who, on commission mainly, though with a small allowance for expenses, ran around the British Isles, boosting a trade paper. That came to an end for all of us in October, and I had to take to the road again selling purely on commission. My line was educational books, about the hardest thing in the world to sell. At times I did quite well at it; at other times very indifferently. In one of my successful periods I, still able to hope, got married. A very severe attack of bronchitis forced me to abandon salesmanship. I tried freelance journalism and for a couple

147

of years made an approach to a living by contributing to the London daily press short articles, ultra short stories and paragraphs to the chatty columns of which most London papers then made a feature. But with the changes of format and policy which came over the English press in the middle 1920s the market for such contributions disappeared and I was unable to find anything else that would set the Linotypes using up lead. I became unemployed. I tried most desperately to get work even as a navvy, but found out that anybody seeking employment as a navvy has to be able to prove he has had experience.

At last in 1927 I hit on something for which inexperience did not disqualify. I became a 'temporary' prison officer. And a rather good one, I was often assured. I liked the job. Indeed, it had a fascination for me, for I was still eager to see life from all angles. I became the friend of murderers, thieves ('screwers' or 'whizzers'), the acquaintance of blackmailers and a host of lesser scoundrels. I'll say little more of the three years I spent in a London prison as a 'screw'. Some time during those years I was sworn to the rigid observance of the Official Secrets Act.

The pay was very low, something like a few bob over two pounds for a fifty-hour week. Consequently, the temporaries, unless they were pensioned ex-policemen, as many of them were, were always on the lookout for something better. Young fellows discharged from the army with very good characters could hope to be advanced to be permanent prison officers. I would have jumped at the chance of doing so, but I was now in my middle forties and too old to qualify for a pension. I had made enemies as well as friends among the prisoners, and for a couple of years I went about London 'with my beard over my shoulder' as the Spaniards say or used to say.

With my usual knack of getting on the wrong bus I left the prison to become a schoolmaster of sorts. In 1930 I got the chance of becoming an instructor, not teacher, mark you, in one of the Juvenile Instructional Centres which the Labour government of that year was, under pressure from the Liberals, setting up for unemployed boys and girls. It would make a not uninteresting tale how I came to get the job. There was behind it a good deal of muscular effort in inducing some young scamps to listen to a talk from me on books they should read. I was acting as a 'substitute' in a library class in the Old Kent Road neighbourhood at the time. The instructor in charge of the Junior Evening School saw the lads listening to me and reckoned it as the most extraordinary thing he had seen in his thirty years of schoolmastering. He was also superintendent of one of these Juvenile Instructional Centres. For over thirty years I had not entertained the notion of teaching but he told me that I should be just the chap for an instructorship in the centre. Qualified college-trained teachers would not, even when offered extra pay, go near the centres, he told me, and the education authority had been sending him along university graduates, whom the boys would hurl to the floor, taking from them the bags of coppers they had been given to pay the fares of the youngsters. He did not think they would put me on the floor. I seemed to have a very unusual power of control over boys. I put on a modest look, keeping silent about the punches on the chins and the clouts on the ear-holes which had persuaded the Old Kent Road youths to listen to a talk from me on Stevenson and Prescott as exponents of adventure in two totally different veins. Would I accept a position as instructor in his centre? The pay would be about twice as much as I was getting as a temporary prison officer. The hours of work would be only fifteen per week. It seemed to me that such a job would leave me plenty of spare time for writing and various other activities in which I was then interested. I agreed to become an instructor. I had an Irish friend already at it, and he described the game as money for jam. I knew it must have been something like that if Sammy Watson could do it. All right: I would be sent for the first vacancy that occurred.

The change from being a 'screw' to being an instructor was not quite so sharp as had been that from being a fireman to starting as a journalist. On late duty on a Sunday evening in the prison, I, in charge of a wing of the prison, saw about a hundred of my criminals composed angelically for sleep before I turned off their gas jets, and at 3 p.m. the next afternoon I took my stand for the first time in a classroom. Forty ragged unemployed lads from the toughest districts of London were seated uneasily on chairs ranged round the walls in front of me. I guessed I was in for a pretty rough time, and my guess was not far wrong.

At that time the Board of Education would not recognise these unemployed centres. There was no syllabus or timetable for them. An instructor was shut in for three hours a day with a bunch of the lads. All an instructor in 'General Subjects' could do with them was to talk to them on something that might be interesting to them and entertaining. Attempts to get them to do any written work had merely resulted in pens being used as darts while the ink pots had been used as ammunition against the unlucky instructors. There did not appear to be any idea of educating these youngsters behind this bunching of them into the centres for three hours a day, alternately forenoon and afternoon; the thing was to keep them off the streets and so impress them that they, not old enough to have the vote, could not have their nine bob a week dole money for nothing.

Well, I had let myself in for it and I must make the best of it. I was introduced to them as a man who had seen a lot of the world and read a lot of history and literature and so would be able to satisfy their curiosity on a wide variety of topics. One boy immediately stood up – I saw to his standing though they forthwith objected that no previous instructor had demanded that of them – and said he had an uncle in South Africa and was thinking of going out to him in a couple of years. What was South Africa like he wanted to know. What industries were there in it? How had it become a part of the British Empire? British Commonwealth of Nations, I corrected him. I managed to keep their attention for an hour by a dissertation on South African history: from the landing there of Van Riebeck to start his vegetable garden, its seizure by the British during the wars against Napoleon and its purchase from the Dutch at the end of these wars to The

Great Trek, the fighting between the Boers and the Zulus and the discoveries of diamonds and gold. In short if I could not tell them a lot about South Africa of 1930, I told them a pretty vivid tale of its past, and the boys seemed fairly satisfied. Then I asked them questions. Why had England fought against Napoleon? Who was this Napoleon, anyhow? Did they know that he had once been a poor, penniless, jobless lad like themselves? They knew nothing very definite about him and agreed to listen to the story of his life. At the end of two hours they seemed to decide that I might be worth tolerating. And so I went on with them, first provoking their curiosity and then satisfying it. The superintendent and the head of the centre, the head of some commercial school in the region, commended me. At the same time I never for three months went in the long narrow passage leading from 'the hole in the wall' or came out through it without having my hand on a truncheon in my trousers pocket. I had minor rows with them. There was a May evening when a squint-eyed young husky stood in front of me swinging a chair round my head and wanting to know what I'd do if he brought it down on my napper. I laughed and told him he'd find my reactions to such treatment rather interesting. He then put the chair to its normal use.

By midsummer we had got them to the stage when we could get them to work with pencils, and a few months afterwards we took the chance of providing pens and ink-wells and desks for them. They took to this treatment very kindly. I was fortunate enough to be able to get jobs for three of the best boys, and thereafter I was their golden-headed instructor.

Meanwhile my ambitions in instructorship had been widened by the education officer, who advised me to try other areas of educational work in which he thought I had ability to succeed. In such areas personality and an ability to become friendly with men seemed to count more than academic qualifications. Men's (senior) Evening Institutes, for instance. I was to apply for admission to the panels for instructors in such institutes. He would back up my application. I got recognised as qualified to teach in them such subjects as

English, English literature, geography, history and public speaking. I had been reviving the old elocution lessons of my Dublin days, had been tub-thumping anywhere I got the chance, and had become a member of several debating and literary societies. It was not, for instance, my fault that the Liberals were not returned in 1929.

A head of one of those institutes offered me the jobs of teaching English composition and lecturing on general knowledge in his particular 'Working Man's University' in 1931. Here again, so an educational expert who claimed to have a big hand in starting such institutes long years afterwards told me, there was no definite idea behind them except that of keeping working men off the streets and so save them from falling prey to the Communists. The classes were mainly for hobbies, boot repairing, carpentry, home decoration and the like. An instructor had to maintain an average attendance of eleven in his class, else it just went phut. And all depended on his power of attracting men. I must admit I had one hell of a job in getting eleven men together for an English composition lesson on a Monday night, and for a lecture on general knowledge on a Friday night. But I managed it, although not always by means of which the authority, had it known my tricks, would approve. Mostly half of my numbers in the evening classes were unemployed lads I had been teaching during the day and who were now so attached to me that they would follow me all over London to any class so long as I paid their entrance fee to it. My evening pay was at first 11/- for a two-hour class. I got such fine written work from my working men that after two years my fee was raised to 16/- a night. And throughout 1931 and 1932 juvenile unemployment rose so rapidly that the centre ran two sessions daily, for both of which I was engaged. In the latter year I was instructing for nearly forty hours a week and drawing down something like twelve pounds a week. Not to be sneezed at in those days. Anyhow, a big advance on the two-pound a week I had been getting as a prison officer.

That there was nothing permanent about it was made painfully clear in 1933, when juvenile unemployment practically ceased to exist, and numbers at the Juvenile Centre got so low that there were only a couple of hours a week available for me. And when the Board of Education finally recognised the centres in 1934 there were no hours at all. For, strange to say, the Board did not think that employed juveniles should be taught English or arithmetic. I had, as a result of this view, a very lean time of it. In 1935, however, I was engaged by the head of a commercial school to teach geography and English for fourteen hours a week, and soon afterwards I was given a start at teaching English in a technical school a couple of afternoons a week. All part-time teaching and, of course, all as an unqualified teacher. I had by this time started public-speaking classes in several other of the Men's (Senior) Evening Institutes all paid at the rate of 16/- a class and so I was again up in the money. I got such good results in teaching geography at the commercial school that after a time I was given history to teach. In 1937 and 1938 I was making as much as seven pounds a week. I would not have been allowed to earn anywhere near as much, for taken annually my earnings were higher than the salaries of most so-called qualified teachers. But my pay claims went into three different departments at Headquarters, and so I was allowed to go my merry way. I had to produce results, of course. I produced them. In the winter and spring, what with piles of homework to be corrected, and I feel sure I was never a day behind in returning corrected work, I had to work upwards of a hundred hours a week.

In the summer I used to take it easier, for there was not near so much homework to set during that term. The examinations for which my youngsters used to contend were over soon after Easter. I had glorious weekends of cricket with a club of some prominence in the Club Cricket Conference circles and became its opening bat. That at age fifty-seven was not such bad going. I did not always get home from a match completely sober.

The Munich scare threatened a sudden ending to this very pleasant world I had built up for myself. Evening classes were, of course, threatened with wholesale closure from the moment war broke out. A scheme for the evacuation of all day schools from the capital had been hastily brought forward. Part of it was that only qualified salaried teachers should go on it. I could hardly grumble about that. Almost all my day classes had been for young people, who came either to the commercial school or the technical school for part-time education; in the former case, the students were probationers for the lower rungs of the civil service; in the latter, trade assistants coming two afternoons a week under a plan by which their employers (a national concern) hoped they were – by giving them the opportunity of further education – increasing their chances of promotion. These youngsters would not be evacuated: therefore, there was no reason for my going either. I had some few classes for full-time day students, but nowhere near enough of them to give me occupation with them if evacuated. True enough, the London County Council at that time offered to make me a salaried teacher, but at a salary much less than half what I had been earning annually as a part-timer. I declined the offer, trusting to Chamberlain and his umbrella, and I don't suppose there was anybody in London gladder than I when that poor muddle-headed old gentleman returned to London proclaiming, however wrongly, that he had secured peace in our time. I could then resume my career of, as it was sometimes officially designated, a peripatetic teacher.

I had that year undertaken to start at a new Men's Institute a class in Public Speaking. The institute was in one of those London districts that are neither aristocratic nor utterly working class, but was a strange hodge-podge of shabby gentility and slum combined. It was about the toughest to get going of all these classes I started, but I eventually got a gooky set of young chaps around me in it. It was, it need not be said, closed down on the evacuation of 1939, but I managed to revive it in 1941 on my own return from evacuation and keep it going till the middle of 1943, when it was eventually closed down because I could not raise my average attendance per night of class from nine and a half to ten. And that at a time when every male able to stand on two legs was being drafted into the forces! It was my last evening class. By then I had been forced much against my will to become a salaried teacher and what with the increase of income tax and the difficulties of travel in the black-out I accepted the closure without demur.

So throughout the winter, spring and summer of 1939 I hared around London to my various part-time day classes, teaching some of them even on Saturday mornings. I would leave home about 8 a.m., getting to the commercial school, in which I always started the day's struggle half an hour before the classes began. On a great piano I laid out my work for these classes so arranged that I never had any fumbling when the youths came in to me. The teacher who has to remove his gaze from students while he is putting away one set of books and getting out another is just asking for outbreaks of disorder, and once disorder starts in a class there is no stopping it. I don't pretend to know at what age pupils acquire a sense of decency of behaviour towards a teacher. I should guess that under our so-called modern education it is somewhere round about the age they have nippers of their own to deal with. I was thus able to watch the kids seat themselves quietly, then order them curtly to get on with their work. I never used textbooks. I was then a bit of an expert in the use of a typewriter and duplicator. I used to cyclostyle (duplicate) all my lessons, some of them in thousands of copies at a time. This was especially so with history and geography lessons, and most always in English too. I'd invent examples for English composition from ordinary life, sentences of English as she is spoken in Walworth, Lambeth or Southwark to be rewritten in standard English.

When they were ready for work, I'd walk round distributing to each pupil a cyclostyled sheet. If the subject were English, he or she had to set about the exercises on it; if history or geography, it had to be copied into a special notebook. This system ensured that least for threequarters of an hour out of an hour's class the pupil was occupied. The homework questions were always set at the foot of the sheet and I had no objection if an enterprising youth took time by the forelock and got on with it.

On Mondays and Fridays I spent the morning at the commercial school and the afternoon at the technical school. In the former I would teach history or geography from 9 a.m. to noon, then snatch a hasty lunch in some working-class cafe, have half an hour's recreation at a crane machine – I had become rather an expert at getting cheap watches and clocks out of them – and then hare across London to get to the technical school, at which I taught English and what was called mathematics, but was really nothing more than simple arithmetic, to the up-and-coming 'Yes, Modoms' of London's stores. That went on to three different groups from 2 p.m. to 5 p.m. At the latter hour I dashed off to get another meal and raced the home-hour rush to get to an evening school in some other part of London for a class from 8 p.m. till 10 p.m. I tried to get to the evening school by 6 p.m. for a number of the adults who came to me for English had taken up correspondence courses, and would come thus early for help with maths papers, Latin papers and the like. I'd get home about 11 p.m. and then perhaps have a couple of hours' preparation for my next day's lessons.

As the war clouds gathered again in the late spring and summer of 1939 and Chamberlain declared he was not taking his brolly places this time, I viewed with rather more equanimity than the previous year the approaching dissolution of my little world. For on the second scheme of evacuation I was to be included at the urgent instance of the head of the commercial school. He reckoned I would be the only one with him who had any knowledge of English country life. Well, I certainly knew how to play shove-halfpenny, how to share my pint of beer with a countryman, tell him to 'drink hearty' from it, hoping he wouldn't, or how to drink hearty from his, if it were proffered me, whether he meant his exhortation or not. There was this snag about my being taken on evacuation: that I would be paid but for twenty hours' work per week. I might do more, and often I did, but I would not get a penny for it. Still, I'd be getting just over six pounds a week, and that was a lot better than having to stay in London and go hunting around for a job at the age of fifty-eight.

I was so sure that this time the patience-exhausted maniac called Hitler would set the world ablaze that in June I packed my three children over to Ireland and in July their mother and I followed them for our holidays. We gathered the children from my various relatives and took them with us for a few weeks to the silver sands of Dundalk Bay. And there one morning with the clouds playing a grand pattern of light and shade over the Mournes the end of my world came with the news in the Dublin papers that Germany and Russia had signed a non-aggression pact. We arranged for the children to stay behind with my relatives and that night my wife and myself took the mail for London. She had a very good post as secretary to the managing director of a London firm. It would evacuate to some place in the Home Counties. That at least was something to know, whereas I had not the slightest idea of what part of the British Isles I would fetch up.

17

As to that particular concern I was left in uncertainty for another ten days, an uncertainty aggravated by the prospect that no matter where I or my wife went, we would in a way have four homes to keep up. My relatives, though comfortable in comparison with what the people of the Baronry of the Fews had been in my young days, would have in decency to be subsidised somewhat towards the upkeep of our children; my wife and I would have to pay for our board and lodgings wherever we went; and there was a home in London to be kept for us when in God's a mercy a way would be open for us to return to it.

The head of the commercial school called a meeting of his staff for the morning of the last Saturday of August. We had to make arrangements for the pupils who would be coming with us on that evacuation, and there then did not seem to be any overeagerness on the part of parents to rush their children out of London. So, all parents had to be impressed on the importance of having their offspring removed out of reach of Hitler's bombs, which were expected to fall on the metropolis within a few hours of the outbreak of war. We had no provision that that amiable individual would fail to act up to the general anticipation of his conduct. The first circular was got out and posted that Saturday forenoon, and on Monday morning some sixty of our girl students and some seven or eight of our young boys turned up at the school with their little rucksacks on their backs. Parents had to be written to again so that we might have their written consent to their children coming with us. Any younger brothers or sisters were free to come along too, and we would arrange for their education at the country schools of the place to which we were going. In this way our party was brought up to over one hundred.

We spent the week waiting for the word to set off to our unknown destination. It was not an idle week. Gas masks for the youngsters had to be adjusted. This task was given over to me as one having had some experience of smoke helmets, and lectures had to be given to prepare them gently for the changes they would find between London and country life: warnings had to be given as to the things that might be done and might not be done in their new environment. Most of that lecturing also devolved on me, but as I was not occupied in class teaching, Headquarters would not sanction a penny of pay to me for all this extraneous work.

On Thursday afternoon we received word that we were to start off the next morning as soon after eight o'clock as we could manage to do so. The youngsters had entered into the spirit of the adventure, and we were at Waterloo a few minutes after eight. With some other school party, which was also rather small in numbers, we were bundled into a train. Even now not a hint was given us of where we were bound.

The train left London as if Hitler's tanks were after it. Its first stop was Salisbury, where some women gave us coffee and cakes; then the train resumed at a more leisurely rate through a rather pleasant terrain in which chalk hills, troop hutments and sad, protesting-looking birch trees had given way to rounded heights, beech or oak covered, and lazily flowing streams that seemed bent on turning back upon themselves. We came to a little junction on the borders of two south-western counties and there heard that that morning Hitler had unleashed his tanks and planes against Poland. Some of us had been hoping against hope that so far the evacuation had been but a try-out of the much heralded preparations, but with the receipt of this news within the hearts of the most optimistic died the idea that we were on a rehearsal jaunt; evacuation was a reality.

We were detrained and packed into buses, in which we were

whirled for some miles through a very pleasant countryside, rather thick with old-world small towns or large villages which seemed asleep in the golden sunshine that had followed a morning shower. We were travelling through Hardy's Wessex, one of the drivers rather pityingly informed me. The buses pulled up in a village on a plateau in what he called Outer Wessex, the scene, he told me, of the commencement of one of Hardy's best-known novels, though the village itself consisted of little more than a square-towered church, just behind which was a rather large provision shop, a drapery shop, a garage and an inn, the signpost outside which invited us to try ——- ales as the very best. A little distance off the road to our left was a rambling one-storey school, not much bigger in all than would be the lavatories of a London school. Close by it was a spacious farmyard, in which a multitude of cows, not driven out as yet after morning milking, wandered about expressing by loud moos their curiosity at the group of bewildered Londoners. By early afternoon the youngsters had been allotted to foster parents, of whom, I gathered from a chat with the village pedagogue, there were two very distinct classes: the toffs (women of wealth and station) and the rubbish (wives of farm labourers, village tradesmen and the few craftsmen who pursued the little village industries precariously surviving from a bygone age). The teachers needed foster parents as well as the children. I thought I was rather lucky in that I was billeted with an ex-lady teacher, the wife of one of several jobbing builders of Bronshall as we had been told the village was named. I had quite a comfortable room assigned me, but it was not home, for I was enjoined to be as sparing as possible of the electric light, and that to a fellow so inveterately given to reading in bed as I was gave me a none too happy feeling. Besides, my wife's firm had moved out of London that same morning. She didn't know where I was; I didn't know where she was; our children didn't know where either of us were. And who knew what the rather chancy possibility of her letters addressed to me care of the London school address being forwarded to this spot in the wilds of Dorset were? The possibility did come off, and afterwards the loneliness was not so great.

Next, it became a question of whether there could be found any teaching at all for me to do. We had not with us enough pupils to keep fully occupied according to educational standards all the permanent teachers who had come with us from London. The result of this was that some of them had to put in part of their time in the village school. Some of them considered this a bit *infra dig.* Our London ladies were mainly subjected to this transfer. They grumbled that the descent from teaching sophisticated London young ladies commercial subjects to teaching yokels the three Rs was degrading them. If the part-time teachers were sent back to London, there would be work enough for them in their proper sphere in the church hall, which, with its adjoining kitchen had been assigned to the evacuated youngsters as classrooms.

Luckily for me, the billeting officer – a charming, if a trifle old-maidish, lady – had billeted our boys on farms a few miles out from the village and, more luckily still for me, the man who, as a part-time teacher like myself, had come down with us from London to continue the training of these boys in rather a narrow line of commerce accepted a full-time job as accountant, secretary or something of that kind with an East Anglian firm. None of the others could replace him, and the local authority could not supply a trained teacher for that particular line. Also no part-timer from London was willing to adventure into the wilds for the small sum to be earned. The boys, in love with their new surroundings almost from the first moment, readily agreed that they should change over from their narrow sphere of training to an intensive course of general education, of which I should take charge.

Then arose the difficulty of accommodation for these lads. There was no hall available in the village for their schooling. Even had there been one there was no transport to take them to it, and so advanced were our ideas about education that Shanks's mare (or one's own feet) could not be entertained as a means of getting to and from it. This problem was solved by a suggestion from me that we should rent a room at a farmhouse central to all the lads. We got one for five shillings a week. It was fitted with electric light and provided with a fire against the cold days of the oncoming winter on the condition that two of the boys billeted on that farm should clean the grate and lay the fire. This the two lads agreed readily enough to do. So on a syllabus designed by myself and covering a course of fairly advanced arithmetic, English, geography and economic history we settled down to a very happy time together. I had had nothing whatever to do with this group while we had been in London, but we soon became friends. They constituted almost the last group of boys with whom I managed to attain what should be the good teacher's ambition: that of being friendly with the youth he teaches.

Part of the time had to be set aside for physical training. That was another thing about which I knew next to nothing, but we got over that by the purchase communally of a football and by my teaching them to play soccer, about which I did know something. Our ground for playing the game was a meadow quite close to the farmhouse, and there we gave one another some hefty knocks with the utmost goodwill.

My time with them was a bit clouded only by the ranging over the countryside of portly educational inspectors in big gallons-to-the-mile cars, who seemed to think that it was of the utmost importance to the country that this rustic academy – Rushe's Academy we named it after the name of the farm – should be closed down and the lads transferred to evacuated schools in the country towns about. The lads refused to be transferred, and the portly gentlemen looked rather helpless.

I took them for but three hours in the afternoon as by some regulation, the reason for which I never could find out, the hours for teaching pupils in this type of school must not exceed fifteen per week. Five hours more were therefore needed to make up my approved maximum of twenty per week. The head provided these for me by setting me to teach geography to the senior girls for one hour each forenoon. I did my best with the little dears, but tossing geographical knowledge to them was much like tossing buckets of water on the walls of a sun-baked house. These young ladies had a wonderful resistance to knowledge of that kind.

However, after Christmas my position with them was somewhat reversed. I was put on to teach them a subject which they were anxious to learn, but which I dislike teaching. And disliked intensely. It was shorthand.

How that came about was through one of the ladies put to fill in her minimum of teaching hours in the elementary school of the village getting her nose up about the degradation she thought this instruction of snotty yokels inflicted on her and declaring her resolve to return to London, where some schools for further education were still working.

In the estimation of the villagers I had registered a score over my London colleagues. In the village lived a youth with his mother. The lad suffered from some ailment precluding his attending prep school for a scholarship examination for entrance to one of the better-known public schools. The mother applied to our head for one of the London pedagogues who could coach the young fellow in Latin, English, maths, geography and history up to the standard of the examination. He needed French, too, but the mother thought she could bring him along in that. I was the only one of the Londoners able to fit the bill for the other subjects. He was a kindly young boy. I used to take him for an hour and a half each morning. So, what with flitting about from his place to the church hall for my wouldn't-learn-geography girls, and getting some lunch and then haring out to the farm to take my boys for general education, I was not exactly standing still. In fact, daily I was covering a goodly distance on a second-hand bike I had acquired in the village.

One morning as I was dashing away from the boy ambitious of securing his public school scholarship and working pleasingly hard for it, I met our head. He stopped his car and beckoned me across the road to him. I thought I was for the last jump.

'You can teach shorthand – the system taught in the school?' he asked much to my astonishment.

I pointed out that it was more than twenty years since I had had any occasion to use shorthand, that that particular system had been much changed in those twenty years and, consequently, I would need months to work up the modernised version of it.

'I can trust you absolutely,' he replied to this. 'Get down to your modernising straightaway. That Miss ———— thinks she's putting me in a hole by going back to London. That I can get nobody to take her place at teaching shorthand. I want you to do it, for the senior girls at all events. Mrs ————- who knows a little about it, can teach it to our juniors. Got money enough to get the books you want? You have? Then send for them tonight and be ready to start teaching it after Christmas. Then she and her career can go wherever they like.'

I sent to the publishers of the system for their most up-to-date books on it, and for the next three or four months had enough to occupy my evenings in my large bedsitter.

The mention of a large room leads to the inference that I had been moved from the residence of the ex-schoolmistress, Mrs Dora Hands. A few weeks were on the average enough to make the Bronshall housewives weary of their Londoners, teachers or youngsters. The good women did not exactly turn us out, though in some cases of the youngsters that is exactly what they did. Rather, they developed mysterious illnesses such as heart strain. Mrs Dora caught that complaint and presented a medical certificate to that effect to the billeting officer. The latter had then no choice but to find me another billet. My first remove was to be to the household of one of the toffs, but when on my way to it I learned that the toff would insist on my dressing for dinner every evening, I pointed out to Miss Fillson that years ago the silver moths in Australia had reduced the only dress suit I had ever possessed to black ash so she had to cry off from that arrangement. She drove me round the village to find some other home in which I would be received. To seventeen different houses she drove me, my

rucksack, my typewriter, my cyclostyle copier and my suitcase –
I had been up to London for a weekend and had lugged all these
back with me to Bronshall – and all seventeen refused to have
anything to do with me. At last she got the wife of the village
coffin-maker to let me have a room. A far smaller room that was
than the one I had had with the retired schoolmistress; so small
that I had only the kitchen in which to sit of an evening to
prepare my various kinds of schoolwork for the next day. After
a fortnight the new foster parent went to Miss Fillson and said
she had a daughter coming home from service in Mayfair. Obviously
I had to set out again on my wanderings. This time I was lucky.
An American lady married to a Scot consented to have me and
allotted me a very large room most comfortably furnished with
bed, desks, bookcases, armchairs and having access by a private
staircase. For a while my meals were brought up to me in that
room by a comely young Jewess, a refugee from Austria, but, as
the Scot and his wife got to know me and make allowances for
my silence and a few other idiosyncrasies of mine, I had my
meals with them. For the rest of my time on evacuation I was
very happy indeed in that room, becoming close friends with my
latest foster parents. To me one great blessing in the remove was
that I could of an evening have the solitude my soul craved and
had access to the Scot's library, a fine collection of over five
thousand volumes, for he was an extern lecturer for some provincial
university.

Here I remastered our system of shorthand, and after the
Christmas recess, during which I had taken back with me a
portable wireless set, I felt quite competent to stand up to the
teaching of it to the future pencil-lickers of London business
offices. And so, I escaped the inspectorial axe until the Easter of
1940. Then my wife and I had the pleasure of a week in Ireland
with our children, one of whom we brought back to London
with us, as my wife's firm had some time before it chucked up
its evacuation and settled down again in its old premises in the
capital.

After Easter, however, things were for a few weeks in a state of ferment. The thing that affected me most closely was that two of my boys had been withdrawn by their parents to start work in London; if the inspectors had grumbled before that six pounds a week was being wasted on having me teach eight boys, they were, I thought, much more likely to grumble now when I had only six with whom to deal. However, they left me in peace. But our head was recalled to London for some scheme connected with the making of munitions in their spare time by employees at Headquarters. The administration of the school thus fell to the deputy head, and a task of an entirely new kind devolved on me.

The previous autumn, swayed by the 'Dig for Victory' slogan then being blazoned abroad, our head had taken twenty perches, in Wessex lugs of allotment from the local district council. Nothing had been done on this derelict and weed-infested ground during the winter; nothing could be done on it during the fierce frosts and snows of that spring of 1940. Friction had already broken out in many small ways between us and the village pedagogue. He was working with the village boys another strip of twenty lugs alongside ours. He complained to the council that the Londoners were allowing their strip to run to waste. I was ordered to take the London boys three afternoons a week to work it.

I had been accustomed to food growing in the South Armagh Rocks, but this allotmenting, in which all work had to be done by the spade and shovel, was a bird of a totally different colour. The plough and horses had been our chief means in the Rocks. And the London lads, though willing enough, far more willing than I as a matter of fact, to take up the task, had to be shown the operative ends of most of our tools. That we got the strip of light clay cleared of its couch-grass, woodbine and dandelion, and in a state of promise of producing vegetables, was, I reckoned, a pretty good piece of work. Whether it was as educational for the boys as authority held it to be is a point on which I have my own doubts.

And in early June, just as nice rows of green plants were

appearing where a month before all had been weeds, the axe came very close to my neck. I got a telegram from London that numbers no longer justified my retention. I thought it rather an odd time for such notification to come, as the deputy had become dangerously ill and for some time I had been doing for him such little administration as the school required. That, I concede, was not very much; mainly some statistical returns to be made in duplicate both to the London and county educational authorities. I prepared them, an easy enough task for one who had won his way through the complexity of army forms, and the sick man, sitting up in his bed of death, signed them, for, of course, as I was but a part-time employee my signature would not have been valid.

One wet Friday morning, I dashed about the village to say farewell to my acquaintances and, intending to catch an afternoon train to London and unemployment, returned to my room to find on my desk another telegram telling me I was to remain in Bronshall. An explanatory letter would follow.

It came a couple of days afterwards. It admitted that I was virtually the acting head of the evacuated school, but I must remain satisfied with my pay for twenty hours a week. Anyhow, though I thought it rather stingy treatment, it postponed that which I above all things dreaded, the starting out at fifty-nine to seek a new job.

The girls were going back to London week by week. Hitler was starting to soften up England by bombing, and the Bronshall district, through which ran several rather important railway lines had an early taste of this bombing. None, it is true, fell near the village, but we had in July some rather startling nights. London was as yet unvisited, and parents, naturally enough thinking their young ones would be safer in the capital than in Dorset, hastened to bring their children home. The few boys stood fast. But at the beginning of August we had so few pupils left with us that it was rather farcical to pretend any longer that we were an evacuated school. And the small number of girls still left with us had, such was the frequency of air raid alarms, to spend most of their time in school crouching under their trestle tables in the church hall to avoid flying glass.

Early in August the London liaison officer drove round and informed me that we must all go back to London. We could fix the date for our return. The girls voted for doing so immediately, but the boys pleaded to be permitted to remain until September 1st so that they could have it to say that they would have spent a complete year on evacuation. The liaison officer consented to this and told me I could treat the remaining time as a holiday, taking the boys about the countryside to show them places and things of interest. He said nothing about how I was to get them around, but they soon solved this problem for themselves by borrowing from the villagers bicycles that were just removed from the scrap-heap stage. My own was not a lot better. Still, we had a merry few weeks of sporting through Dorset.

On September 1st, 1940, just as Hitler was commencing the attacks on London I brought the lads back to it. When we saw the destruction already wrought in the outer south-western regions of the capital, we had an eager wish to be on the way back to Bronshall, but our fate was no longer of our choosing. We got into Waterloo just as the siren wailed out its warning. The Underground was shut: we had to hang around its passages for some hours till the 'All Clear' sounded. As I got to the door of my home, there was another alarm, and I had scarce time to drink a cup of tea before I was hurried to a neighbour's Anderson shelter. And the same on Sunday night and for that matter for many nights thenceforward. On the Monday I crawled out of the shelter to start the search for another job. It did not seem a hopeful search.

18

Nor was it. The laughter caused employers by an old, grey-headed, baldy fellow asking for work is something that still rankles.

When I had been a couple of days on this bitter search, I had a card from the head of the commercial school asking me to call in and see him. I was more than delighted when he put before me his plans for restarting the school in London. Would I accept an engagement for twenty-one hours a week? My job would be teaching shorthand mainly, with a little English thrown in. I accepted with alacrity.

We had to go off to Headquarters to get the approval of the inspector of commercial schools for this arrangement. That gentleman was for a time rather hesitant about giving his assent. I could furnish no certificates to prove that I knew anything about this art of strokes and dots. Finally he consented that I should have a bash at teaching it on the grounds that I had taught a number of other subjects very well and had never let the authority down. But I would be very closely watched.

Unfortunately I wasn't. There was no time in which to watch me. The Blitz on London was just then working up to its full intensity. Apart from the night raids which so much disorganised London transport that the pupils found the utmost difficulty in getting to the school and invariably came very late, the siren was wailing almost continuously throughout the day so that we had to spend most of the school time in the school basements. That they were not much of a shelter was shown in the middle of September when the school was struck by a bomb one night and hundreds of the public who had sought shelter in them were killed. Anyhow, the day before it had been decided that the school must be closed down, so irregular was the attendance at it both of students and staff, and the government had given notice of withdrawing its probationers. That night our home with hundreds of others in our district was smashed-up by a parachuted naval mine: the office in which my wife worked was wrecked by another mine. On the whole, September 18th 1940, was a cheerful day for me. The consoling thing about it was that through people fleeing their wrecked homes about me I fell into the occupancy of a separate Anderson shelter, which I fitted up till it was admitted to be one of the most comfortable in London.

I restarted the search for work. The only thing I could find to do was checking of figures for a firm that specialised in the issue of dividend warrants for companies with a large number of shareholders. It was in its way childish work and wretchedly paid, a whole day at the soul-searing task fetching me in but what two hours of teaching would have done. Still, it was memorable to me as the only one of the many jobs I have done from which I got the sack. A few of us had stayed behind one Saturday at lunchtime to fill in the amounts on a batch of these blasted warrants. There happened to be a typewriter lying idle in the office in which we worked. Partly, I suppose, to show my cleverness I thought it a bright idea to fill in the amounts on the typewriter, I was getting on like a house on fire with the job, filling in twice as many as anybody else when in to us stepped the man in charge of the job. His breath showed that he had lunched well. He had with him the young dame whom office scandal asserted to be his choice concubine. And, of course, he was anxious to show off his importance. He ordered my instant departure so and my not returning. I again became an inspector of buildings.

In a modified form evening classes were being restarted on Saturday afternoons and Sunday mornings. I dashed around to see whether I could restart any of mine. But all but one of the school buildings in which I had held them were now filled with trousered beauties of various sections of the Civil Defence Service. I got going again the one I had originated at the time of the

Munich crisis, and with that one class a week I had to be content until the beginning of 1941. I had plenty of time for digging up from lea the allotment I had been assigned on a London common. Numbers of old buffers were similarly engaged. I saw in it at the time as I still see in it an act of faith on our part that England would surmount the perils by which she was faced in that winter. Seemingly unhindered, the German planes were weaving nice patterns of vapour trails in the cold air above us as we dug.

As the man who had so unceremoniously fired me from the warrant checking had in the meantime been called up – the poor devil was killed some time later while he was piloting a bomber over Berlin – I got another spell at figure checking at the turn of the year. And just as it ended, I had cards from two heads of evening institutes inviting me to call to see them as they had a novel and interesting plan to put before me. This was no less than that the morale of people in public shelters might be uplifted by their having lessons in public speaking and debating. Three of the shelters it was proposed I should tour on this course of uplift were in the Old Kent Road region; two of them the basements of factories, the third the crypt under a church. Trustworthy men who would not cheat the educational authority were required, as there would be no registers of the classes kept. I was taken around to see these three shelters and have a look at the prone population from which I was to attract my classes. I felt on seeing them that a fellow who could give instructions on how to pick winners or fill in football pools correctly would have an immeasurably better chance than I with my tuition in stance and voice production. The fourth shelter offered much more promising material for my *métier*. All four, however, yielded reasonably commendable results. Usually I was able to get about twenty or thirty of the shelterers into a corner round me, though the lessons tended to become rather lectures by me on current events than attempts by a sorely stricken people to climb the hills of oratory. As the year advanced into March and April, the folk tended to be later and later in coming to the shelters; and my performances were rigidly scheduled as to take place between 8 and 10 p.m. Some of the folk I had undoubtedly interested, but generally I had to concede that the shelterers as a whole were not deeply interested in uplift of a mental kind. And how could they? They would leave those basements and crypts in the morning not knowing whether their humble homes had or had not been levelled during the night.

It seems rather mean to mention the matter, but it is a fact that for the most of those excursions in uplift I, desperately needing the money stated on my engagement forms, was not paid anywhere near in full. The amount I was shortchanged came to some four or five pounds, and often in these past few years I could have found use for this money.

Because of the inadequacy and uncertainty of public transport I, after the first few nights of uplifting, preferred to trust myself to my old bike. On these rides to and from the shelters I kept a sharp lookout on the winter sky for the bursts of anti-aircraft shells. When they seemed to be producing momentary stars directly overhead, I would jump off the machine and dash for the refuge of the nearest doorway while bits of shrapnel and pieces of shell thudded on the highway. Good luck for me in that though I often rode eight or ten miles through London on these nights of minor blitzes no bomb ever fell near me.

In March, 1941, I most unexpectedly got back to day teaching. A telegram from Headquarters advised me to report as soon as possible to a large London technical school. Early the following forenoon I propped my bike outside its imposing front and by a kindly porter was shown into the office of the principal, a most imposing sort of man. As do all those in educational authority, he had first of all to lecture me on the importance of his establishment. I knew that gambit by this time: another way of lecturing me on the importance of himself. For all that, he turned out to be a kindly man and my very good friend. He has been dead for some years now. Peace to his dust!

The situation, I was at length given to understand, was this.

The school was made up of three distinct sections: a daytime senior department for young men being trained for the executive flights of the trade taught in the school; an evening section or evening class for men working at the trade but ambitious to soar a bit higher in the hierarchy of the manual worker; and a junior section in which, from the ages of fourteen to seventeen, school-leavers from elementary schools got a preliminary drilling in the various handicrafts embraced in that trade or became qualified as young office workers to be kicked about by the executives. A man was wanted to teach English up to matriculation standard to these juniors, give them a good sound grounding in social and industrial history and geography, a smattering of the dismal science, economics in other words, as well as a grounding for the first-year boys in maths. The two regular masters for these subjects had some months before joined the forces; substitutes, science teachers, I gathered, who had taken over the subjects had just been taken on as backroom boys into various ministries. Very desperately was needed, therefore, a part-time teacher who could acquit himself in all these subjects. English literature had to be taught as well and a love for it ingrained in the hearts of the young tradesmen. If I could prove that I could teach all these things, the job was mine.

Except in maths I had references to show that I had taught them pretty successfully. And I was able to convince both the principal and the head of the junior section that I knew enough maths to have a bash at teaching that subject too. So I came away from the building with an engagement form for as many hours a week as would bring me in seven pounds, which would have looked small to me a few years before but in the altered circumstances seemed to me a fortune. The pay was 8/- per hour; if there was a waiting period between classes, and there often was, I got less an hour.

The junior section, I learned during my first few days, was but a substitute for the real junior section which was still away on evacuation with a full staff of trade and academic teachers somewhere in the South of England. My section was for boys whose parents had withdrawn them from evacuation or boys who, having left elementary schools still operating in London, wanted our particular branch of technical education and did not want to go on evacuation. It was not, therefore, very large, having only about thirty-eight boys all told, spread into three groups.

I found, too, the cackle about English and English literature up to matric standard a bit of eyewash when I came to look through the youngsters' exercise books. The only English they appeared to have done was some dictation exercises, and the only English literature the writing down of the dates of birth and death of a few of our more classical authors with lists of their works. They let me know vociferously that most of the geography they had done was the learning whence had come a few of the materials used in their trades and the colouring in of outline maps run off on a rather shaky shapograph. In history, I was told, one boy read out aloud from about the dullest primer of economic history I have ever seen – and by heck! I have seen some dull ones – while the others blew bullets of chewed paper at one another.

They did not like my proposition that they would have to write essays of their own, and would have to copy into special exercise books my versions of geography and economic history. There were three or four large cupboards of English 'readers' in the room. The practice, I gathered, had been to sling out to the youths the keys of these cupboards and let them browse as they willed among these 'readers'. I would have none of that. There was much glaring by them at me and by me at them.

In those days I could glare very well. I proclaimed my charter of freedom for them: they could do what they liked so long as they did what I told them to do. And, oddly enough, we got along quite harmoniously on these lines.

In the second year there, there came in a large number of recruits so that in the first year's group I had upwards of eighty, and eighty in a class is a number that takes some handling. For most subjects they were divided into two classes, '1X' and '1Y', but occasionally I would have to take the two classes together. That was, needless to say, in English lessons. We'd then move into the largest classroom in the school, and even at that there'd be lads trying to write on window-sills and on the tops of cupboards. And many of them would be doing it not at all too badly. The principal and the head of the junior school let me get on with it, for they said I knew what I was doing and English was being really taught for the first time in the school. Quite a part of the time allotted on our timetable for English was spent in debating. Boys were learning to keep minutes of their meetings, and other little things of that kind gave them an interest in their classes. I hope some of the lads arrived at the futures I often pictured glowingly for them, those of being secretaries of district branches for their trade unions and perhaps going even higher in the hierarchies of trades unionism.

My teaching hours increased to nearly thirty a week. With the increase in them my earnings rose to a point where they exceeded the maximum salaries of full-time qualified teachers. Of course that sort of thing had to be stopped. And stopped rather abruptly it was. I was made a full-time temporary teacher on a yearly salary of three hundred pounds, about half what I had been earning annually as a freelance. At the same time I was notified officially that I would have to have assistants. Against that I had for long struggled, probably from some vanity as well as from cupidity on my part. I was not very fortunate in the early assistants, who were men close on retiring age and held that no amount of hard work on their part would increase their pensions by a stiver. Besides that they were inclined to resent as *infra dig* their being put under the tutelage of an unqualified teacher such as I was. Our relations were not always exactly friendly. At last there was sent along a keen young Welshman with no illusions about his dignity and eager to absorb any tricks of the teaching trade that anybody, qualified or unqualified could show him. We became close friends, and it became rather a joke that in an English school English was being taught by an Irishman and a Welshman.

Soon afterwards according to the custom then in force I, having two assistants, was given some special title, which brought me an annual grant of some forty pounds above my pay. For all that, it rankled not a little in my mind that I was tutoring men (who were getting at least twice as much in salary as I was getting) in the know-how of putting English subjects across to boys who did not want to know them. Yet for all that we got on very happily together and were on the most affable terms up to the end of the war and indeed after it.

With the implementation of the Butler Act, a much vaunted piece of legislation, leaving everything much as it was but calling it by a different name, we became a secondary school of some kind, technical secondary, I think. Staff increased, especially on the trade side, though even on the academic side there were additions in that some of the regular staff had to lend a hand in the teaching of English classes. Such men were usually mathematicians or scientists, excellent fellows in their own subjects, but not all divinely inspired in the teaching of English and not at all anxious to have anything to do with it. One year, I remember, I had to set the line by which eight of these should hoe, and what little gifts of diplomacy I had were strained to the utmost.

Apart from the ever-increasing number of recruits joining us at the commencement of each scholastic year, the autumn of 1945 brought us still further accession in that the evacuated section of the junior school then rejoined us. Some of them were fine lads. There was one, I recall, who might have developed into a second Robert Louis Stevenson: but I suppose that poor, grubby misfit of life is leisurely pushing a barrow round London streets shortly after 8 a.m. and during the day is a keen supporter of snack bars and cafes. Others were not so fine, having a good conceit of themselves and needing very much the application to them of the old Roman motto, *debellare superbos* (to overthrow the proud).

The end of the war too brought us the resurgence of the mania for sport during school hours, the utter boloney about its developing team spirit, sportsmanship and the now somewhat debunked attribution as to the winning of Waterloos. We had been spared all that during the war, as the school sports ground had been in occupation of the army.

The return of the evacuated section also brought us a new headmaster for the junior section, an admirable man, with a tail to his name of degrees and diplomas in this and that, but without any much capacity for the handling of boys. He was also a keen subscriber to the doctrine, utterly mischievous, in my opinion, that the more interests youth are given, the better for them. Authority seemed to think that if a bunch of young fellows are sent off to picture galleries or to concerts or theatres in school time, they will work so much better on their return. I, professing myself an utter barbarian in art and music, was called upon only to escort the youngsters to theatres in the daytime and I admit that such escorting was a pleasant way of being paid for work. The shows were usually given by fifth-rate repertory companies in the dingiest of suburban theatres; the plays given were generally ultra highbrow. What benefit the young devils gained from these jaunts I never could establish.

I am no fanatical believer in homework. It has its benefits, though I am quite aware that a very good case could be, and often is, made out for its entire abolition. There remains a nagging insistence by school authorities that it should be set, and in a school such as ours there was every reason why it should be set and done, especially in the winter and spring. Up to the end of the war we had been getting it done reasonably faithfully and well, but the termination of the war put an end to that. Youth movements of all kinds – youth clubs, cadets for this, that and the other thing – sprang up all over London. The young lads were encouraged to join such organisations, many of which were not anywhere near as uninteresting as they were made appear. Teaching for a teacher who wanted to see youths' mental powers developing became rather comparable to the Irish vulgarism of micturating against the wind.

Apart from that there was the unease caused by the fact that under the new Act all teachers had to be able to show college certificates of training or be holders of degrees from a British university with a teaching faculty. The only chance of escape for a buffer like myself who for nearly twenty years had been earning plaudits as a teacher was in a clause stating that an unqualified teacher recommended as having over a number of years carried out teaching duties for a local educational authority would be accepted as qualified by the Ministry of Education. In our school there were no less than twelve of us, eleven of them trade teachers, who were unqualified according to the provisions of the new Act. We all in a joint letter and with the support of the local authority for our application asked for recognition as men who had for long periods given complete satisfaction in our work. The trade teachers were recognised; I was at first cast into outer darkness.

I was over sixty-five then and was being kept on as head of the English department year by year at the special request of the authority to the Ministry. I was occupying what in the jargon of the 1944 Act was called a responsible position and was getting a generous yearly bonus for occupying it. I fought the case with the panjandrums of Whitehall. I was warmly supported in that fight by the inspectors of the local authority. About a year after the battle was reopened a lady inspector came along to try me out both in the theoretical approach to teaching and the handling of youths in a classroom. She was a gracious woman. I don't know which of us left the other more puzzled, but the Ministry relented and at the age of sixty-seven I had the satisfaction of being recognised as a qualified teacher. There was but empty self-satisfaction in that. It did, I admit, add a few pounds a year to my salary and afford me the satisfaction of being able, without feeling ashamed, to listen to the chatterings of colleagues who were ever seeking to evoke memories of their days at 'coll' (training college) or at a university, generally some rather undistinguished modern one, but a university all the same.

In these post-war years I was blessed to this extent: that more than half my classes were made up of young fellows who had a

180

direct interest in securing what general education they could. They were youngsters who had to pass an external examination regarded by the associations connected with their trades as equivalent to the matriculation. This examination was nothing like the matriculation, but it did require a slightly, very slightly, advanced knowledge of such English practices as paraphrase, precis and analysis of sentences. The drilling of these practices into the heads of lads of seventeen and eighteen who in their twelve or thirteen years at elementary or technical schools had never heard even of the parts of speech, was like teaching the lads how to make bricks without straw. Still, the consoling thing was that the young fellows did try to make the bricks, straw or no straw.

The classes, which in those closing years of my pedagogic life it gave me the greatest pleasure to take, were classes of trade apprentices who came to school one day a week under a scheme fostered by their trade associations. They should have been the most difficult classes of all to handle, and most of the other teachers having to do with them regarded them as one of the things sent to try pedagogues. I got on very well with those boys. As one of them wrote about me, I was the greatest affliction of all to them for I knew all the answers.

These apprentices at first thought that a rather scurvy trick was being played on them in their being sent back to school when they had for three or four years been looking on themselves as almost men. After some rather lurid exchanges with them, during one of which I remember standing with clenched fists in a doorway and inviting a husky fellow to come and do his worst, they settled down quietly enough with me and turned out some really good work in the way of English compositions. And they were not sneakish or insolent.

I stayed on as long as I was permitted to stay. I had never come within the scope of the superannuation schemes: I did not come even under the scope of contributory old age pension. Every July all the staff would assemble in the staff room to hear our stocky, grey-haired principal speak on his behalf and ours the stilted farewells of the educational world to its faded-out warriors. I used then to feel that my own turn for these laboured eulogies could not be very far off.

I was nearing sixty-eight and feeling the strain intensely, and there had been several times symptoms of approaching breakdown, though for the reasons already stated, I could not afford to take notice. Eventually it was conveyed to me that the local authority could not see its way to asking the Ministry of Education to allow me to stay on any longer. I trust I showed a stiff upper lip, but I gulped all the same.

So, towards the last days of July, 1949, I sat in the staff room and heard my valedictions uttered. The principal said I was a man of exceptionally strong character; I had crowded into a few years more teaching experience than most men had acquired in a lifetime of it. He hoped a way might be found in which my great gifts for teaching and my experience in it might even yet be made available to the school. I was, as a matter of fact, offered some evening classes in English. Desperate as was my need, I declined the offer. I had been taking these very classes for three years and had been climbing sixty-one cemented steps to get to the eyrie in which they were, and would be, held. Every climb the arteries in my calves had been threatening to burst. I said I was beyond the age for mountain climbing and in any case it had always been for me a case of '*nulla vestigia retrorsum*' (no stepping back again). I hope the college-trained pundits understood that. I was mad enough to buoy myself with the hope that even at sixty-eight I might find some sort of employment through which I could buy myself my cigarettes.

Inasmuch as I was being paid for the holiday period, I could postpone the time for that search. I decided that as it was likely to be my last long holiday I would enjoy it. I selected a curious form for that enjoyment: I went with my neighbour on a cycle trip from London to South Wales. Food and lodging proved almost impossible to obtain en route: we half-starved and slept rough for several days and nights of it, and I came back to London more dead than alive.

The quest for work provided several employers with amusement. The gospel of men working on till they were seventy had not then been preached by the politicians. And my rather half-hearted attempts to secure work ended almost as soon as they began. One day while I was riding my now motorised cycle along the streets of our suburb, the world suddenly became very dim around me, and I pitched off the machine onto the kerb. Some women out shopping disentangled me from it, gave the obvious advice that I should make my way home as quietly as I could and call in the doctor. He came next morning, applied some strange-looking instruments of his art to me, tested reflexes and then said:

'You've had it, lad!'

'What?' I asked.

'Cerebral thrombosis,' he replied. 'If you take things very quietly, you may recover. But no more tearing about on allotments; no more rushing around after rabbits.' I had all the war years been an unduly enthusiastic allotmenter, and as if that, combined with my teaching and fire-watching almost every night (I held some post which meant that my neighbour and myself were about in every alarm) were not enough I had added rabbit keeping to my activities, and it proved about the most arduous of the lot.

I took his advice and for some time seemed to be recovering fairly well. My left hand was practically useless: the greater part of this text was lying about in manuscript, and I beguiled the time by typing it out one-handedly. And, as the Irish scribe annotated marginally in the text he was copying, that has been a weary task, and, very probably, quite a fruitless one.

The doctor sent me to the physiotherapy department of a large hospital, where I was most thoroughly vetted by one of its experts, called, I understand, consultants. Nothing much the matter, he assured me. Just a touch of residual rheumatism, the usual after-effect of a stroke. A little heat treatment and a little special exercise would set that right in no time. I got a few touches of the heat treatment, practised the prescribed exercises faithfully and was certainly making quite a lot of improvement, so much so that I managed a visit to the Mournes, cycled and walked quite a bit in that delightful country.

Soon after my return to London something happened quite suddenly one evening as I sat by the fire. I just seemed to go all to pieces, I could scarcely breathe because of an intense pain in the region of the heart. So, I went back to the physiotherapist, hoping to meet the gracious young consultant who had taken such pains with me on my first visit. Alack! It was quite another type of man. 'No more exercises,' he laid down dogmatically. 'What you need is a thorough medical overhaul. I'll fix up an appointment for you tomorrow with the medical people.'

And when I had hobbled that far on the morrow a very youthful consultant, sitting never nearer to me than five yards, delivered himself thus:

'Heart weak. Go home and lie in bed.'

I did not exactly go to bed, but I kept very quiet for a couple of months. Then, when the warm weather of 1951 came belatedly along, I struggled down again to the doctor and laid my woeful case before him.

'Heart!' said he, feeling my pulse. 'Nonsense, man! Your heart is far stronger than mine is. That pain's nothing but a trifle. Here,' tossing me a prescription, 'go to any chemist and get these drugs. Chew one whenever the pain becomes really bad.'

As time went on I got from him prescriptions for several other kinds of drugs, each one of which would relieve me of this, that or other pain. I'd stand a very fair chance of winning the drug swallowing championship of London over the past twelve months.

Lately I have been recommended to go to another hospital, in which the treatment of all kinds of rheumatism and arthritis is made another speciality. Another consultant. 'Nothing the matter with you,' said he. 'Hands and feet a bit stiff, eh? We'll soon unstiffen them.'

I'm back to exercises, light treatment, vibrators and such things. And not one of them has discovered that my trouble is one for which, I understand, they have no remedy. And if they gave me time to tell them, they would just pooh-pooh me.

Daily, my joints stiffen. One doctor told me the best cure for me would be to win a first dividend in a Treble Chance Pool. I think it would have a wonderfully bracing effect, and it's not for want of trying that I lack its benefit.

On most days of the week I report to the hospital for one or other of the various forms of treatment. There I chat with 'anatomies of death', in-patients in much worse case than I, men and women in wheelchairs which they never leave unless when they are lifted from them.

Some days when the sun shines in the summer, I would hobble as far as our local common to chat with these other anatomies of death, old men, who, like myself, hang on pathetically to the feeble sparks of life left in them while they still make gallant effort to put the bookies out of business.

Until lately I fondly cherished the hope that I might again see the summer sunlight and cloud shadows dance along the slopes of Slieve Gullion or see its serrated summit, knife-edged against a rising moon, that I might once more sit in the cabin in Carnally Rocks, hear the rumble of the fan-bellows as they send the flames whirling round the kettle and hear a gentle Carnally voice bid me: 'Sit over now an' have a sup iv tay.' That can never be. The voice is stilled. '*Ma chandelle est morte.*' There is nothing left for me but to live as far as possible in The Communion of Saints for I recognise that the moment cannot be far distant when I will hear 'The Call of my People' to join them. And though it will not matter where I rest the long rest, it saddens me to think that that rest will not be in Glassdrummond or Creggan or, what would be closer still to my heart's desire, alongside the bones of those grand men of God who struggled so hard to guide my wayward youth. And it saddens me still more that I am left to wonder if any of my own family will pause to say, 'God have mercy on his soul!'

All Saints' Day, 1953.

185

Carnally Calls!

School days gone forever,
Strange emotions that I feel,
Time to take on life's big challenge,
Put one's shoulder to the wheel.

Winter time was nearly with us
Sky was dark and full of rain,
Said goodbye to friends and loved ones
Caught a bus then took a train.

Belfast docks so dark and dismal
As I stood there all alone,
Feeling old and brokenhearted
Never been so far from home.

Figures rushing all about me
All their faces looked the same,
Silent, tall, a ship was waiting
Duke of Argyle was her name.

Towards midnight, siren wailing
Slowly moving out to sea,
People waiting at the quayside
No one there to wave to me.

Speed increasing, sailors shouting
As we sail into the night,
Everywhere a touch of sadness
As the land fades out of sight.

Heysham harbour, dawn is breaking
Step ashore with case in hand,
Get a glimpse, the first of many,
England's green and pleasant land.

Smell of smoke and noise of engine
As this land we travel down,
Through the window see new places,
Stafford, Rugby, Kentish Town.

Euston fogbound, black and ugly,
Take a tube to Gloucester Road,
Streets round here appear much brighter
Are they really paved with gold?

Find the hotel, meet new people,
Have some lunch and hide the grief,
Food is different with such strange names
Yorkshire pudding, sprouts and beef.

Go to work on Monday morning
Just like being back at school,
Overwhelmed by new surroundings,
They must think I am a fool.

Try to mix and talk to others
They say it's easy if you try
But I'm not sophisticated,
Very green and very shy.

Get a letter Tuesday evening
Family gossip, questions, fears
Read it over in the bathroom
Eyes are brimming full of tears.

Christmas party, music, dancing
Lemonade that tastes of beer,
Funny how I'm feeling dizzy
Is one still a prisoner?

Go to see the sights of London
Piccadilly, Leicester Square,
Think about the square in our town,
Wish I was walking there.

Going back home for Christmas
To that little bit of heaven,
Feeling happy and much brighter
Than in London, southwest seven.

Holiday is almost over
Only wish I could remain,
But I must again face London
All that loneliness and pain.

Settle down into a routine,
Very often when alone,
Wonder what the folks are doing
Back there in that childhood home.

Weeks go by very slowly,
Then the months turn into years
But always still I hear the echoes
Of the home town in my ears.

Happiness is only fleeting,
Holidays that come and go,
I know that England's not my future,
So why I stay, I'll never know.

Life is very complicated
London full of pain and strife,
Can I ever leave this city
Go back to the simple life?

Wish I'd never made this journey
Never had to emigrate
But I know I will return there
For even now it's not too late.

The Old Carnally Road

The best road is the old road that through Carnally runs;
It crosses bogs and climbs up braes
No hill it ever shuns,
They drove it straight as a ramrod, from Tharles to
    Johnny Quinn's
And if left to itself for a couple of years
'Twould surely get lost in whins.

On the roads of half the world in a wandering life I strode
But I'm happiest when I'm travelling on that Old Carnally
    Road,
That Old Carnally Road, that Old Carnally Road,
Sure I'm happiest when I'm travelling on that Old
    Carnally Road.

The best road is the old road that through Carnally runs
And it's often I raced along it to Grants for a couple of
    buns,
And slow I trudged along it to McDonnell and his school,
For McDonnell was a good man who over us ran the
    rule.

On the roads of half the world in a wandering life I strode
But I'm happiest when I'm travelling on the Old Carnally
    Road,
That Old Carnally Road, that Old Carnally Road,
Sure I'm happiest when I'm travelling on that Old
    Carnally Road.

The best roads are the old roads that round Carnally run
And may I be carried along them when my pilgrimage is
   done
On the shoulders of the neighbours to rocky
   Glassdrummond grave,
While my prayers rise up to Jesus that He my soul will
   save.

On the roads of half the world in a wandering life I strode
But I'm happiest when I'm travelling on that Old Carnally
   Road,
That Old Carnally Road, that Old Carnally Road,
Be the last of all my journeys on that Old Carnally Road.

Carnally's Heather Bells

Back again in smoky London, from my window I look
  out,
And the strips of London's gardens, their vain beauty to
  me shout,
But my eyes stray far beyond them to those hills above
  the dells
That's clad in purple glory in Carnally's heather bells.

Kindly people bid my greeting as I pass my fretful way,
And I make them answer scarcely noting what they say,
For the voices I am hearing, quaint old words like 'ans'
  and 'ochs'
Come from friendly people calling around Carnally's Rocks.

London's left me not unblessed, I have much to glad the
  heart,
Health and home and work for doing and some scope to
  play my part,
But there comes those soul-sore moments, when this town
  and all its stock
I would gladly barter for one acre of my wild Carnally
  Rocks.

The Road Above Belurgan

I've travelled many a highway stretched wide from town
 to town
They're as smooth as any table, no uphill or no down
Their cambering is perfection and their drainage is an art,
But that road above Belurgan is the road that's in my
 heart.

That road above Belurgan is like a switchback rail
It has hairpin bends and turns just like a crooked nail,
Its drainage is just nature's and it's rough in every part,
But that road above Belurgan is the road that's in my
 heart.

Ach! I'm over here in London a-knocking down the
 Strand
And the ladies they be withering me with looks so proud
 and grand,
I'd rather fix my eyes upon a girl not half so smart,
On that road above Belurgan that's forever in my heart.

And when it comes to dying and the Soggart's at my ear
And he's whispering of paradise in tones I scarce can hear,
And I'll want to go to heaven in the slowest ass and cart
By that road above Belurgan that's forever in my heart.

Carnally

You are heading for Carnally, John,
My soul with envy fills,
For the youth that's strong within you
Will be striding o'er the hills.

You will stand on Creggan-Howard
What a scene will then unfold
With your eye full of the world
As an ancient poet told.

Cuchulain's noble mountain
Will lie purple in the sun
And lesser mounts will seaward slope
In arc to Dalgan's Dun.

As if to reach to Cloggerhead
And guard the sleeping town
As if and with God's benison
The dappled skies look down.

West and north will range your vision
Sweeping round Collon's trees
Taking in the rich Louth cornfields
And the diamonds of the leas.

And Monaghan of the little hills
Mount Egish and Black Bank
And the speckled mountains of Armagh
That stand like troops in rank.

You'll go down the brae by Donnelly's well
The Donnelly's glories fled
Springing Pat and supple Annie
Long, long since have both been dead.

Of that clan now left but Alice
Knarled as a churchyard yew
Ah! The bright-eyed smiling Alice
Fifty years I knew.

Take a turn out by the Creeckan
Where the Campbells once were strong
Poor Nancy dried my childhood tears
With story and with song.

Their little homes in ruins now
Where many a winter's day
They put life back into me
With a well-stewed cup o' tay.

Wander out the winding valley
Round by Tavey's and McShane's
Where to homes amid the heather
Led away by twisted lanes.

Down by Reel's and Campbell's bog-holes,
To the savage 'Creg-a-Dill',
Where the rain gives voice to lilting
Of the streamlets round the mill.

O! The Hills around Carnally
They come surging through my dreams,
I see Carnally's barren Rocks
Its bushes and its streams.

And I pray that those who live there
From sorrow have release
As I pray that those who die there
May rest in God's sweet peace.

Moyle's Mill

Moyle's Mill they say is a lovely spot
Where the larks and linnet sing,
Where the salmon and trout do sport about
Together in one string.
There is a lovely place beneath the old mill-race
Where my heart with joy does fill,
I love to walk and have a talk
Around by Moyle's old mill.

Of beauty rare none can compare
It's the sweetest spot I know,
With its meadow green and the old mill stream
Where the Fane doth gently flow.
Where'er I be on land or sea
My thoughts will come back still
To that dear place of matchless grace
Around by Moyle's old mill.

If around that way you chance to stray
In the months of May and June
When the fields are white with daisies
And the trees are in full bloom,
To hear the thrush on a hawthorn bush
Some joyful hearts to fill,
You'd enjoy a day if you chance to stray
Around by Moyle's old mill.

Appendix

THE DAILY NEWS, LTD.

TELEPHONES
CENTRAL 5000 (40 LINES)
ALL DEPARTMENTS CONNECTED.

TELEGRAMS
STAR, LONDON.

The ✦ Star

YOUR REFERENCE

OUR REFERENCE

BOUVERIE STREET,

LONDON, E.C.4.

G.B.Tyson, Esq.,
Publicity Dept.,
County Hall.

March 20th.1935.

Dear Tyson,

Thanks for your note, and here is Mr.

P.K.Murphys M.S.B.

I have tried several people with it; they
all say the same thing; that it is too sordid, depressing,
and as such is better left unsaid. I disagree. It can be
stated without over-statement and without being rubbed in.

The only channel I can now think of would be
to try the editor of a new monthly called " The Humanist
Gazette," Fulwood House, Fulwood Place,Holborn, W.C.

With best wishes,
Sincerely,

Spencer Jones.

Hampton Court Palace

All communications should be addressed to—
" The Master.

11 April

FROM THE MASTER,
1 PETERHOUSE,
CAMBRIDGE.

Dear Murphy,

I can not tell you how really touched I am at your very kind letter — "feel — thank you very much — is quite inadequate — but both my wife are indeed grateful for your kind words which we appreciate more than I can say. I never fail to realise how far fortunate beyond my deserts I have been with my wife with me all these long years though they seem more like 25 than 50 — Then too I can never forget those best of fellows my old B.I.F. comrades throughout the last Great war. I tried to say something of my feelings for them in "Finalli & Gown" I am so glad you like my only attempt at literature. The King was good enough to write me a

a personal letter for writing it + said
he thought every officer should read it
you are quite right in what you say of
the Leane brothers – they were great – then
Raymond I knew much best. I went
specially to see him in Adelaide. I only
heard from him last week – some time
he asked me to be Hon. Col. to his old
Guard in S.A. I'm so glad to
see what you say of Maclagan
say I know he will like to know
I am telling him – a real good officer.
25 April 15 seems a very long war
off now – but they were great days &
I really enjoy hearing from one who
was there. I much hope I
may meet you at Anzac Day same.
If you are there do please be sure
to come along & speak to me.
All good wishes & again Thank you.
Yours sincerely. Birdwood of Anzac

A.I.F. FORM No. 535.

AUSTRALIAN IMPERIAL FORCE.

391

Department of Repatriation and Demobilisation.

Application for a Discharge in a Country other than Australia.

UNIT *Australian Army Ordnance Corps (Seconded to Branch 4 D)*

NO............ RANK *Lieut. (T/Capt)* SURNAME *MURPHY*
(In block letters).

FULL CHRISTIAN NAME *Peter Kevin*

PRESENT LOCATION *Branch 4 D, 54 Victoria Street*

1. I, the above-named member of the Australian Imperial Force, do hereby apply for my discharge in *United Kingdom*

2. In consideration of my application being granted, I hereby release and discharge the Commonwealth Government from all obligations in respect of my return to Australia.

3. Reasons for application *All my relatives are resident in United Kingdom, family affairs and interests urge my remaining in United Kingdom. Mother, Uncle and Aunt have died within the past four months and the estates of the latter two in which I am one of the heirs at law. I'm interested are not yet wound up. Also to pursue my career as journalist I desire to remain in England. Prior to Jan I was only resident in Australia for 3 months. If repatriated to Australia, I should have to return to United Kingdom*
(To secure favourable consideration these reasons must be stated fully and frankly. If this space is insufficient, a signed statement is to be attached.)

4. Signed at *London* this *eleventh* day of *July* 1919

Name. }
Rank. } Signature of Witness.
Col
R & D Dept. Unit.

Signature. *Peter Kevin Murphy.*

The applicant's signature must be witnessed by a General or Field Officer or Chaplain of the A.I.F.

5. List of references and supporting documents attached (if any).

6. Medical category *A.I.*
(To be vouched for by C.O. of applicant.)
Initials of C.O.

7. No. of entries on Conduct Sheet *NIL*
(To be vouched for by C.O. of applicant.)
Initials of C.O.

8. Length of service. Joined the A.I.F. on *19.8.14*
Total *4* years *321* days.
Initials of C.O.

9. Paybook No. *50877* Deferred Pay due to date £ *164 - 10 - 6*
(amount in words) *one hundred & sixty four* pounds *ten* shillings *six* pence.

10. Commanding Officer's remarks and recommendation.
I certify that the particulars set forth in paras. 6, 7, 8 and 9 above are correct to the best of my knowledge and belief. The application is *recommended* recommended for the reason that *having no long personal knowledge of the applicant I know the statements made for the applicant correct that if any should settle in UK* Signature.
Rank.
4 D R & D Dept.

11. Decision of Director-General, Repatriation and Demobilisation.
APPROVED

Lieut.-General.

12. Action taken
FOR DIRECTOR GENERAL REPATRIATION AND DEMOBILISATION.
DATE *30 JUL 1919*

NOTE.—Units forming part of a Division will forward this form through Divisional H.Q. to the Dept. of Repatriation and Demobilisation, A.I.F. In the case of Units *not* forming part of a Division, the forms will be forwarded direct to the Repatriation and Demobilisation Dept., A.I.F., 54, Victoria Street, London, S.W. 1.

204

CARNALLY ROCKS

D.B.

BASE RECORDS OFFICE, A.I.F.,
7th April, 1920.

Dear Sir,

I have much pleasure in forwarding hereunder copy of extract from the Sixth Supplement, No 31684 to the London Gazette, dated 12th December, 1919, relating to the conspicuous services rendered by yourself whilst serving with the Australian Imperial Force.

x   x   x   x

CENTRAL CHANCERY OF THE ORDER OF KNIGHTHOOD.

"THE KING has been graciously pleased to give orders for the following promotion in and appointment to the Most Excellent Order of the British Empire in recognition of valuable services rendered in connexion with the war, to be dated 3rd June, 1919 :-

To be a Member of the Military Division of the said Most Excellent Order :-

Lieutenant (Temporary Captain) PETER KEVIN MURPHY. "

x   x   x   x

The above has been promulgated in Commonwealth of Australia Gazette, No. 30 dated 25th March, 1920.

Yours faithfully,

Captain P.K.Murphy,M.B.E.,
  C/o Mrs. R.Murphy,
    Carnally,
      Ballsinil,
        County of Dundalk,
          IRELAND.

Major.

Officer i/c Base Records.

PETER MURPHY

4.A.

7th August,   9

TO WHOM IT MAY CONCERN.

                This is to certify that Peter Kevan MURPHY,
late Lieutenant, (Temp Captain), A.A.O.C., has completed 5 years,
45 days service in the Australian Imperial Force, and has resigned his appointment in consequence of being Demobilised, with
effect from 5th October, 1919.

                The following is an extract from his records :9

Enlisted in A.I.F.	22.8.14.
Embarked from Australia.	24.9.14.
WOUNDED.	25.4.15.
Admitted to No. C.G.H. Mena.	13.7.15.
Taken on Strength of Ordnance Corps from 9th Bn.	15.8.15.
Promoted Staff Sergeant.	1. 2.16.
Embarked overseas per "Euripides". Alexandria.	10.5.16.
D.O. 3/21E is amended to read:- Promoted Conductor W.O. Class 1. Substantive Rank.	20.9.16.
Brought to notice Secretary of State for War. Valuable services rendered in present war.	24.2.17.
To be 2nd Lieutenant to complete establishment.	1. 9.17.
To be Lieutenant.	1. 12.17.
Brought to notice Secretary of State for war. Valuable services rendered in connection with the war.	20.8.18.
Attached to Repatriation and Demobilisation Section, London for duty.	18.11.18.
Lieutenant. To be Temp/ Captain.	1. 1.19.
Seconded as Staff Officer Branch 4.D.4 to retain the Temp rank of Captain whilst so employed Repat and Demobilisation Dept.	18.11.18.
Appointed Staff Officer Branch 4.D. Ordnance Repat and Demob Dept.	28.1.19.
Resigned appointment from the Australian Imperial Force in consequence of being Demobilised with effect from 5th October, 1919.	

                                    Lt. Col for
                        Director General Repat & Demob.
                            Australian Imperial Force.

206

FROM **TOOWOOMBA CHRONICLE** W. H. GROOM & SONS LTD.
Proprietors

PUBLISHED DAILY

UP-TO-DATE & RELIABLE.
FOR ADVERTISING THE MOST
PROFITABLE MEDIUM.

Address for Business Communications
" The MANAGER "
Address for Literary Communications
" The EDITOR "
TELEPHONES :
Business Department. No. 16
Literary Department. No. 178.

Margard Street
Toowoomba

B

June 4, 1920.

Published DAILY
in the
**Darling Downs,
West and
South-West,**
which comprises the
CITY OF TOOWOOMBA
and Districts of
Wyreema
Cambooya
Allora
Roma
Warwick
Crow's Nest
Kingsthorpe
Pittsworth
Goombungee
Greenmount
Southbrook
Millmerran
Oakey
Cambooya
Cooyar
Drayton
Dalby
Tara
Bell
Kaimkillenbun
Acland
Goondiwindi
Warra
Surat
Yeulba
St. George
Haden
Charleville
Jondaryan
Clifton
Kulpi
Mitchell
Miles
Yarraman
Jackson
Gatton
Helidon
Westbrook
Hampton
Nobby
Jandowae
Wallambilla
Pickanjinnie
Meringandan
Dulacca

Mr. P. K. Murphy,

Dear Sir,

    I have very much pleasure in giving you a testimonial. You were employed in this office on the literary staff. When the war broke out you volunteered for active service, and was accepted. While you were in our employ you carried out your duties most satisfactorily. So well that we kept your place open for you should you have returned to Queensland. Apart from the patriotic motive that prompted you to resign, your efficiency alone would have secured a position again on our literary staff. Should you gain employment on any newspaper, or any other work, whatever duty is assigned you I feel sure that you will carry the work out with credit to yourself and advantage to your employer. I can safely recommend you for employment.

        Yours Sincerely,

        H. L. Groom

    Managing Director.

James Murphy d. 1899
m. Rose Carragher d. 1918

Peter b.1881 d.1954 m. Ethel (Monica) Gillings d. 1979	Mary d. 1966 m. Pat Keenan d. 1949	Jeremy b. 1884 d. 1966 m. Elizabeth Garvey d. 1965	Lizzie b. 1885 m. Thomas Keenan	Kate b. 1887 d. 1963 m. Andrew Hanna d. 1969	Paddy b. 1888 m. Brigid McParland	Annie b. 1890 d. 1968 m. James Conlon d. 1964
Sheila Rosaleen	Margaret	Jem	John	Charlotte	James	Mary
Peter Brendan	Mary	Pat	Kitty	Mary Rose	Patrick	Rosaleen
James Ciaran	James	Owen		Elizabeth	Hugh	Peter
	Owen	Rosie		Andrew	Jack	Mary
	Rose	Barney		Patrick	Pete	Michael
	Mary	Lizzie			Rose	Catherine
						Paddy
						Anne
						Barney
						Eithne
						Rita
						Brendan